◈ DESTINATION: ◈
BUTTE, MONTANA

This Thursday is NICKEL DAY at COLUMBIA GARDENS
5¢ 5¢
ller Coaster rides 5¢
irplane Spin rides 5¢
rry G 5
FREE
TO AND F
(THANKS TO
16 te inte
COLU
FOU

COLLEEN CLANCY HANSEN

Mountain Pine Press
ISBN 10: 1-59152-141-6
ISBN 13: 978-1-59152-141-9

Cover drawing by Thomas Patchett
Cover design by Kathy Springmeier
Sweetgrass Books
Helena, MT

Thomas, Dylan, from *Under Milk Wood*, copyright ©1952 by Dylan Thomas.
Reprinted by permission of New Directions Publishing Corp., 1.

For more information, email: colleenclancyhansen@gmail.com

This book's content is based on the author's perspective and interpretation
of the subject matter. Neither the publisher nor any associated parties shall be held
responsible for any consequences arising from the opinions or interpretations expressed
within this book.

Published by Colleen Clancy Hansen with Mountain Pine Press

www.mountainpinepress.com
Helena, Montana

Printed in the United States of America.

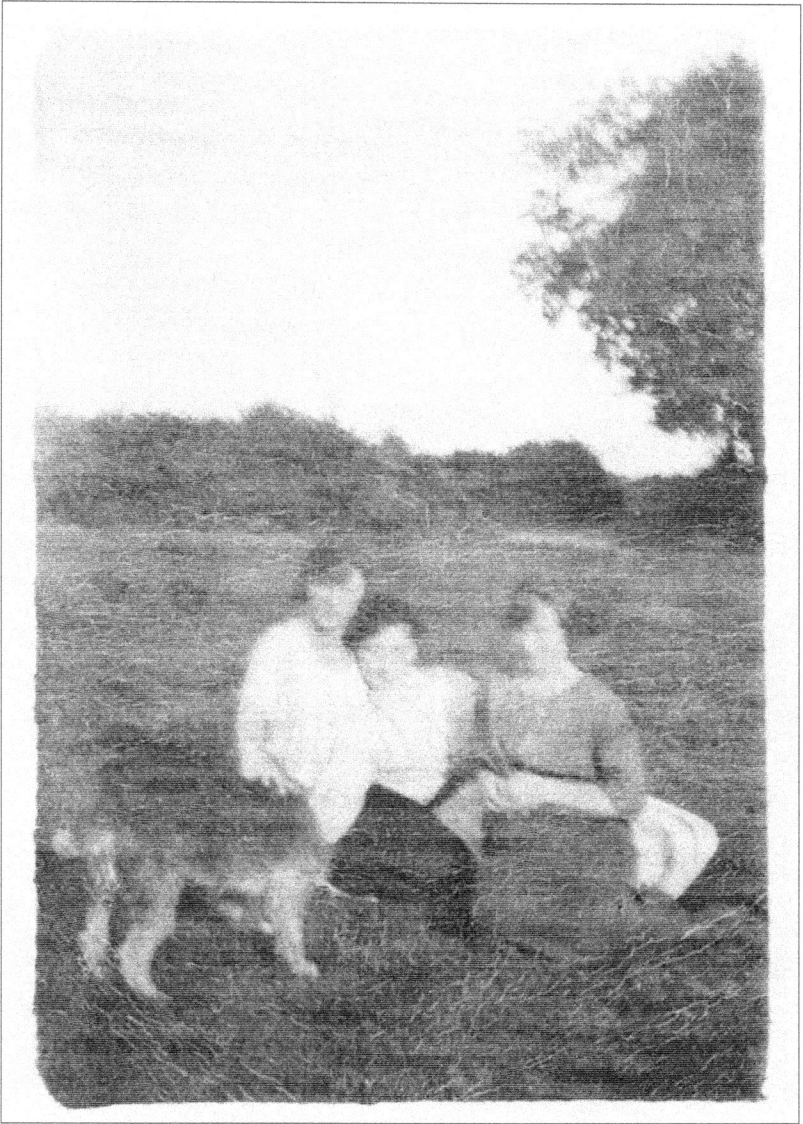

THREE FEMALE RELATIVES IN WALES

THE JOHN, DAVIS, AND CLANCY FAMILY TREES

GREAT GRANDPARENTS FROM SWANSEA, WALES:

Elizbeth Lloyd —m.— William Lloyd   Thomas John —m.— Janet Reese

Margret Lloyd —m.— John John
(1837- 1906)   (1837- 1891)

Elizbeth John	Cathrien John	Margaret John	David John
(1859-63)	(1862-1863)	(1864-1938)	(1866-1954)

Sophia John	Jenet John	Thomas John	Rachel
(1869-1916)	(1872-1966)	(1875-1944)	(1878-1880)

GRANDPARENTS:

Margaret John Davis (Williams) —m.— William Davis
(1864-1938)

Selwyn (Syl) Davis │ William Davis

Adeline (Hattie) Davis Clancy   Florence Davis Cigliani   Thomas Davis

Selwyn —m.— Rose   William —m.— Clara

Rosemary   Joan   Sylvia   Billy   Gordon

(Uncle Tommy) —m.— Ernesta   Florence —m.— Charlie

Joyce   Janet   Leonard   Elroy

GRANDPARENTS:

John Daniel Clancy from Galway, Ireland —m.— Ellen Casey Newman

Adeline (Hattie) —m.— Daniel J. Clancy

Margaret   Florence   Dorothy   Danny   Adeline

FOREWORD ᘓ

ᘓ

"To begin at the beginning. . ."[1] to quote the Welsh poet, Dylan Thomas, is to begin to understand a family where no portraits were displayed, no family stories were told, and no grandparents were still living from whom to glean personal histories. So I begin this story with two bare facts: My father's mother, Hattie, loved marigolds (I, too, love these dazzling, pungent flowers); and she was not Irish. Hattie Davis Clancy had been born in Wales.

This is the story of three immigrant families—the Johns, the Davises, and the Clancys—whose lives intertwined in Butte, Montana, in the late 1800s. It was an exciting time in a boisterous community full of colorful characters. I'll tell this story, then, as both memoir and historical fiction, based on the available facts of my ancestors' toils and joys, but with the immediacy of imagined dialogue and daily life to better capture the essence of the people and the events that shaped their lives.

My father's maternal grandparents, the John and Davis families, were the first members of the Clancy-John-Davis families to enter the United States. They arrived in Butte, Montana, prior to the beginning of the War of the Copper Kings. So, the story begins. . . .

PART I

CHAPTER 1

THE JOHN FAMILY MOVES FROM WALES

A sound in the dormitory brought Danny back to the reality of his new home. He could hear his three-year-old sister, Adeline, across the hall in the girl's dormitory. The oak lockers and seats should have muffled the laughter, but his ears were keen. When Adeline stopped laughing, Danny's attention returned to the John family Bible opened before him. With a finger, he traced his mother's relatives on the family tree written in the Bible's front sheets. This was the John-Davis branch. It was like a prick in his heart to think of his mother and her family.

Danny's mother's grandparents, John John and his wife, Margret Lloyd John, eagerly planned to leave Wales for new opportunities and new memories. Married in March 1859, Margret and John's first child, Elizbeth, was born in December 1859. In 1862, Cathrien was born, but both girls died, Cathrien in April 1863 and Elizbeth the very next month. Both girls were buried in the family plot in Swansea, Wales. Six more children followed: Margaret, David, Sophia, Jenet, Thomas, and Rachel, all born two or three years apart. Then suddenly, the youngest, Rachel, took sick and did not live to her third birthday. John and Margret held the hands of their living children as they prepared to depart Wales in 1880.

Packing everything away for the journey had seemed to be so much work, but it didn't last as long as Margret, who was reluctant to leave her homeland, hoped.

Margret's mother, Elizbeth, had given them many Welsh flannel quilts, including the red and black flannel one that she had just finished sewing. The women of Wales worked on careful stitching, not fancy designs. Margret placed these carefully in the trunk. The warmth would be comforting in the cold winter.

Their small country, Wales, was a mere 130 miles in length. Margret John thought sadly about the famous castles that she now might never see. The English had kept the aggressive Welsh preoccupied with building castles instead of plotting battles. Margret had hoped to make excursions with the children to show them their country's more than 500 castles, but the time never seemed to be right.

She wanted to show them the burial site of the magician Merlin, and she wanted them to see Snowdon with its 3,500-foot summit. It was said that Snowdon was watched over by King Arthur and his knights. Margret imagined hiking to the chair of Idris, in Welsh, *Cader Idris,* a mountain peak where a mythical giant was said to recline while stargazing. Legend held that "anyone who found the actual chair and slept in it overnight would wake in the morning as either a poet or a madman."[1] Afraid of such a serious choice, Margret had never made the trip.

She thought of all the animals in her country. There were said to be more sheep than people. There were the small Welsh ponies, which David and Thomas loved to ride. The children's favorite birds were the puffins and the red kites. Sadly, the family dog, a Pembroke corgi, Wort, would remain in Wales with Margret's mother.

When the time came for the ship to depart, Margret's eyes lingered on the men fishing in their basket-like coracles on Swansea Bay as they had for hundreds of years. Pondering all she was leaving, Margret took some com-

COFRESTR DEULUAIDD (LLOYD-JOHN MARRIAGE CERTIFICATE)

COFRESTR TEULUAIDD

GENEDIGAETHAU.

Elizbeth John the Doughter of John John by Margret his Wife Was born the 8 of December in the year of Our Lord 1859 at 8 aclock P M

Cathrien John the Doughter of John John by Margret his Wife Was born the 30 of January in the year of Our Lord 1862 at one aclock a m

Margret John the Doughter of John John by Margret his Wife Was born the 5 of March in the year of Our Lord 1864 at two aclock a M

David John the son of John John by Margret his Wife Was born the 4 of November in the year of Our Lord 1866 at 9 aclock P M

Sophia John the Doughter of John John by Margret his Wife Was born the 1 of July in the year of Our Lord 1869 at 2 aclock P M

Jannet John the Doughter of John John by Margret his Wife Was born the 29 of March in the year of Our Lord 1872 at 8 aclock P M

Thomas John the Son of John John by Margret his Wife Was born the 6 of March in the year of Our Lord 1875 at 4 aclock P M

COFRESTR TEULUAIDD (JOHN FAMILY TREE)

JOHN JOHN, ELIZBETH LLOYD, MARGRET LLOYD JOHN
IN WALES, THE FIRST DEPARTURE FROM SWANSEA

fort from the thought of the quilts stored on the boat in their trunk. They would serve as a loving tie to home.

Their Atlantic crossing was uneventful, and the ship docked in Baltimore. The family walked to an address John held in his hand. Until they got established, they would stay with old friends, the Higgs, who had settled earlier in Baltimore. The city was large and smoggy. The smelters thronged with energetic men, but John was a hard worker and knew he would prove his strength. Forced to leave Wales by a mining slump, he intended to earn every possible dollar in this new country.

John soon learned that the smelters did not enforce safety measures. Within a year of finding work, he suffered a terrible accident and lost much of his right arm. John was left with a painful stump, but he refused to dwell on the possibility of never working again. With five children and uncertain prospects, a move back to Wales seemed wise. Back across the ocean they went. Margret's aging mother, Elizbeth, was pleased to see them again and to have all of this excitement in her quiet house. The children were happy to see old friends, and Margaret, the eldest daughter, soon married a Welshman, William Davis, a smelter worker.

The John family and the newlyweds spent many "knitting nights" together. As a common pastime in Wales, people gathered around a fire and knitted and entertained each other with stories about fairies and bogles (ghosts).

Despite the familiar comforts, life in Wales remained a struggle. William Davis found work as a smelterman, and his earnings provided barely enough for the entire family. Within a year, however, another slowdown at the smelters forced John and William to consider leaving Wales to find work. Once again, the John family, with Margaret and William Davis in tow, left Wales for better opportunities in America. During the long sea journey back to America, David, Thomas, and their sisters met other children on the ship. Speaking English interspersed with Welsh, they mingled with Irish children. The Irish were even more anxious than the John family to leave their homeland. Many Irish openly hated the English, while the Welsh were more forbearing. Dire poverty existed in Ireland, and those families were thinner, but their children were also more exuberant than others on the ship. Children played quiet games when the seas were smooth. The mothers talked with other mothers from their own countries.

One evening, as they stood on deck in the dim light of a crescent moon, Margret asked John about the wisdom of this move. John thought it would be an adventure. He commented no further, because he was so relieved to have a short time to stop worrying about the next week, or the next month, let alone the rest of their lives.

The destination for the John family and their son-in-law, William, was Granite City, Illinois, just across the Mississippi River from St. Louis. When they arrived, they discovered that no one would hire John because of his severed arm. Their son David, being young, liked his chances in Granite City and vowed to stay.

The John family now included three children, a married daughter, and her husband. They left Illinois for Butte, Montana. This destination was not as unlikely as it might seem. An old friend of John's from Wales, Augustus

CERTIFICATE OF NATURALIZATION.

In the District Court of the Second Judicial District of the State of Montana,

IN AND FOR THE COUNTY OF SILVER BOW—ss.

Hon. _____ _____ _____
_____
Judge Presiding.

In the Matter of the Application of

Wm Davis _____ *an Alien,*

To Become a Citizen of the United States of America.

In Open Court this _____ day of _____ A. D. 189_

IT APPEARING TO THE SATISFACTION OF THIS COURT, by the oaths of _____ Wm Rees _____ and _____ F C Davis _____ citizens of the United States of America, first duly sworn and examined, that the above named applicant is a native of _____ Wales _____ and has resided within the limits and under the jurisdiction of the United States for the five years last past, and in the State of Montana for the year last past; and that during all of said five years' time he has behaved as a man of good moral character, attached to the principles of the Constitution of the United States and well disposed to the good order and happiness of the same.

AND IT ALSO APPEARING TO THE COURT, by competent evidence, that the said applicant has heretofore, and more than two years since, and in due form of law, declared his intention to become a citizen of the United States of America, and having now, here, before this Court, taken the oath that he will support the Constitution of the United States of America, and that he doth absolutely and entirely renounce and abjure all allegiance and fidelity to every foreign Prince, Potentate, State or Sovereignty whatsoever, and particularly to _____ VICTORIA, Queen of Great Britain and Ireland and _____ Empress of India, of whom he has heretofore been a subject.

IT IS THEREFORE ORDERED, ADJUDGED AND DECREED, that the said _____ Wm Davis _____ be and he is hereby admitted and declared to be a citizen of the United States of America.

Signed _____ Wm Davis _____
Signed _____ _____ Judge.
Applicant.

WILLIAM DAVIS'S NATURALIZATION CERTIFICATE

Peters, was the supervisor of the Parrott Mine. Augustus promised that the family would feel welcome in Butte. The city of Butte was growing, and Augustus boasted of a community pride there that the John family had not seen in Baltimore or Granite City.

After so much uncertainty, Margret felt genuinely excited for the first time since leaving Wales. She finally could say to herself that she wanted to try a new life and see new sights. They went by trolley to the train station in St. Louis for their ride west. The train station shone. The brass was polished and the floors were swept clean. On board, Margret thought the compartments would certainly have impressed her mother. Leaving St. Louis, they rolled through new terrain. The colors on the vast plains reminded Margret of Wales. Then came the mountains—massive and seemingly endless! The mountains in Wales paled by comparison.

Late in the afternoon on the fourth day of the train ride, a loud whistle signaled the depot in Butte. As they stepped off the train, they noticed the chill in the air. The depot in Butte was a large, ornate building and was well kept. Mountains encircled the city, including high peaks with year-round snow.

Locals crowded the depot, greeting newly arrived family and friends. Butte residents were stylishly dressed. Women wore large, beautiful hats. One woman's blue velvet hat featured huge pink roses and a black veil. Margret longed to wear such a hat someday. One fashionable man wore a Homburg hat, a new fad sweeping Europe.

Thomas and his sisters were quieter than ever as they glanced around at the line of people purchasing tickets. They sensed the restless excitement shared by all in the Butte, Montana, railway depot. Perhaps the most excited of all were Margaret and William Davis, who were eager to begin their own family in this new place.

THE JOHN AND DAVIS FAMILIES IN BUTTE

N ow the newcomers had to settle in. Each nationality in Butte seemed to have its own neighborhood, Margret's Welsh friend, Lala Peters, advised her.

The Cornish lived in Centerville, "along Center and Main Streets."[1] The Finns "settled in Finn Town, developed along East Granite, Broadway and Park Streets."[2] The Irish lived in Little Ireland, which was located in Dublin Gulch and the Hub addition.[3]

Italians lived in Meaderville[4] east of town, while the French lived in String Town near Brown's Gulch to the northwest.[5] The Lebanese could be found "in the Cabbage Patch mostly on East Galena and Mercury Streets."[6] "The Welsh didn't have a district of their own but were scattered throughout the town."[7]

The Chinese had their alley located "off Main and south of Galena Street."[8] However, "Not all of Butte's Chinese lived in China Alley. Washey washey houses were scattered about the town."[9]

The Butte Miner, one of Butte's newspapers, ran a story about a man named Fun Gee who ran a laundry in Dublin Gulch. Margret read the clipping that Lala had saved.

"Fun, the pioneer of Dublin Gulch laundry man, has left for the Orient on a visit. Wealthy and generous he will be missed in Butte. It was as king of the Chinese, 'washee-washee' houses, that he acquired his wealth.

"A white widow of Dublin Gulch with about ten small children was in competition with Fun at one time—or was she: The lady wasn't physically strong and frequently became ill. Whenever this happened her competitor, Fun Gee, sent his men over to her house to do washing, wringing and ironing and distributed dimes and quarters among her children."[10]

Thomas and his sisters were amazed by the size of Butte. Thomas had been hired to work as a nipper—a miner's helper—and both John John and William Davis worked underground in the Leonard Mine.

The John home was on Yew Street, just up the street from Meaderville, originally an Italian neighborhood that now included some Irish and Welsh. Almost 1,000 people resided in the winding community where small wooden houses sat on narrow streets. Most of the families had some chickens, pigs, and cows that could often be found wandering the streets.

"Backyard gardens provided potatoes, broccoli, garlic, and tomatoes. The women set out white tablecloths for Sunday dinner, but during the week they set out patterned cloths. Family-style meals include appetizers, such as: salami, olives, cheese and anchovies."[11] Minestrone soup was followed by lettuce or dandelion salad when it was in season. The dandelions were carefully washed and gently chopped. Fresh hard-boiled eggs were grated on top of the salad and then drizzled with sweet wine vinegar.

Restaurants like Bonino's Italian Cafe at 116 East Park Street frequently advertised "Are you tired of the ordinary restaurant menus? Then try our Real Italian. . . . Everything to eat and drink—."[12]

Thomas, Jenet, and Sophia enjoyed living in Meaderville. The bocce alleys—there were forty-three!—provided many games for children and adults.

Thomas tried to explain the game to their mother. "Sometimes bocce is played with partners, but you can play it by yourself. The game is played on a floor or alley, a hard surface six feet wide and ninety feet long. Each player uses two light steel balls. Another smaller ball, called the pallino or jack, is rolled down the alley to be the target. The players take turns rolling their balls down the alley toward the jack. The winner is the player whose ball is closest to the jack at the end of the game."[13] Margret shook her head, barely able to follow her son's animated account. "Have fun!" she said with a smile.

The Johns also enjoyed the many culinary offerings found in their new home. Jenet's and Sophia's favorite treats were torchets—braided sugar cookies. Thomas loved to eat lunch at his friend's house because Mrs. Costello bought delicious breadsticks from the Meaderville Bakery.

Something even tastier—though not for young palates—could be found in the Costello basement, where open barrels lined the rooms. Some were used for the grapes to ferment; others were sealed for aging and preservation. A small still produced the grappa, "the eye-opener," for weddings and funerals.

The wooden floors in the Guido Brothers Market were covered with sawdust. "Dominic and Guido . . . specialized in making pork and beef salami, and sausage. A skill learned in their native town of Luca, Italy. It hung on two by fours. They had a certificate of exemption which allowed them to sell anywhere in the United States."[14]

A dark shadow soon fell upon these happy times. John John became ill and died after a three-week bout with bronchitis. It was a sad, frightening time for the family.

William Davis worked in the Leonard Mine, and it fell to him to provide for his widowed mother-in-law and sisters-in-law as well as his wife. Thomas was living on his own, but he helped as best he could. The family's happiness was soon buoyed, however, when Margaret and William Davis welcomed their first child, Selwyn, known affectionately as Syl.

Although she missed her husband deeply, Margret kept herself busy with her daily routine. Other distractions could be found in the busy mining town. She eagerly watched construction on the building on the corner of Broadway and Washington. It wasn't a castle like the one she remembered from Wales, but it certainly looked like it came from a fairy tale. The Chateau, as everyone in Butte called it, was an exact replica of a chateau in Europe. Charles Walker Clark, the eldest son of W. A. Clark, had it built for his wife, Katherine Quinn Roberts Clark. The exterior was made of brick and sandstone. It had a slate roof and, from the mines, copper rain gutters. Margret especially admired the ornate, black wrought iron entryway.

The Chateau was nearly completed in 1898 when Mrs. Charles Clark decided to host a costume ball. Margret was not invited, but her Welsh friend, Lala Peters, was. Lala made plans to wear a national Welsh costume of "a long full-skirted black dress, worn with a black-and-white checked apron, a big white collar (such as Puritan women wore), a white kerchief over the head, and on top of that, a high-crowned black hat."[15] As Lala left for the ball, she promised to give Margret a full report.

The next day Lala was bursting with news. "The Chateau's entryway is grand. All of the ironwork was crafted in Butte. There is a brick foyer with two grinning plaster gargoyles. The octagonal room is on the left. The turret is made of satin wood. The color is like warm honey. There is a portrait of Charles's brother, Paul Clark, by Royal Daulton.

"The staircase was carved in place from African mahogany."[16] The ballroom is on the fourth floor. It is paneled with hand-planed California redwood. The hand-stenciled wallpaper shows Pocahontas and John Smith, and there is another scene of a French hunt.

Lala said she was the only person in full costume. Katherine Clark wore a beautiful white lace gown and on her head, a tulle hat. The red ribbon and white plume were gorgeous in Mrs. Clark's dark, uplifted hair.

By the time Lala finished her report, Margret felt as if she, too, had danced the night away at the Chateau ball.

CHAPTER 3 ৯৯

MARGRET JOHN AND MARGARET DAVIS RETURN TO WALES

I n due time, Margaret Davis was pleased to discover that she was pregnant again. She hoped for a daughter to join their young son. In the fifth month of her pregnancy, the family received a letter from Swansea, Wales. Her grandmother, Elizbeth, was seriously ill, and she wanted to see both Margret and Margaret. As both women quickly packed, Margaret and William talked about a possible name for the second child; Syl was to remain in Butte with his father and his aunts.

Although the reason for the visit was a worrisome one, Margret was glad to return to her homeland. Her two previous departures had been so hasty. This trip would give her the chance to store every detail of Wales in her memory.

When they reached home, friends met them and took their bags along the cobbled streets. As they entered the thatch-roofed home, Elizbeth was asleep by the fire; she had a quilt wrapped around her thin legs. She quickly sensed her daughter,

21

Margret, and her granddaughter, Margaret, and slowly smiled with her eyes. Elizbeth immediately sensed that she was going to be a great-grandmother again. Margaret said she hoped for a daughter this time.

Margret asked Elizbeth how she had been managing to take care of herself and her cottage. Elizbeth said her friend, Maive Jones, came over twice a day to help her get up and walk to the water closet.

Margaret Davis served tea and was glad to sit down. She had forgotten how tired she felt during pregnancy. She'd wake up with boundless energy, but after three hours of work, a rest was needed.

The Evans family, three doors down, was determined to comfort Margret John and her daughter during this difficult time. The Evans planned a trip to Snowdon; they said it was beautiful and both women must come. Elizbeth, too, insisted they go. Margret agreed after she noticed that her mother's cheeks had some color and she had eaten two small meals the previous day.

The group took a train to see the peaks. It would not be a quick journey, but Margret wanted to see again the golden light that surrounds the tallest mountain in Wales. Margaret Davis drank in the smells and sounds and frequently spoke to her unborn child about Wales.

They were invited to the presentation ceremony of the Eisteddfod, a kind of poetry competition. The tradition of the Eisteddfod came from the ancient druids. An archdruid who was surrounded by poets led it. "The band of judges is known as the Gorsedd of the Isle of Britain. The formal rules for the writing of poetry include twenty-four meters of heroic odes. A crown was given for the best free meter poem."[1]

The trip was a bright spot for Margret and her daughter. Their smiles did not last. Only fourteen days after their arrival, Elizbeth passed away. Margret was deeply upset since Doctor Lloyd Williams, her mother's doctor, thought Elizbeth would live for four more months. Margret regretted taking time for the trip to Snowdon, but the doctor assured her that Elizbeth had been able to see Snowdonia's beauty through Margret's eyes.

After Elizbeth was laid to rest, the two women accepted invitations from old friends to go to the seashore, where they watched the cocklers bring in fish. The 2,000-year-old design of the coracles well served the many fishermen in their solitary occupations. Margaret had time to read poetry from

HATTIE'S BABY PHOTO IN SWANSEA, WALES

books in her grandmother's house, and she frequently wrote to William and included a note to Syl. Her body had not grown much, but the oval had descended slightly. This required more trips to the water closet than usual, and she was growing restless for the baby's birth.

Before she left for Wales, Margaret and William decided if the baby were a boy, his name would be William. If the child were a girl, they agreed to name her Adeline, but she would be called Hattie, a derivative. Hattie sounded more casual, more American.

Dr. Williams came to help with the birth. The delivery was really quite easy, thought Margaret. With the birth of Syl, her mother and William had watched her so carefully she felt embarrassed that it took so long. This time she sent a neighbor for the doctor when she was certain there would be a short wait; she knew the baby had dropped, and she was ready for the birth.

After the birth, neighbors sent food, and Margaret took Hattie to be photographed. The cream-colored folder for the portrait was stamped Swansea. After four months, Margret John, Margaret Davis, and baby Adeline (Hattie) Davis left Wales for their home in Butte, Montana.

CHAPTER 4 ᔈ

ST. DAVID'S FEST IN BUTTE

———————————————————————— ᔈ

As the years passed, the John and Davis families grew, and Margret John was a frequent grandmother. She received much-welcomed letters from David and Mary Elizabeth John from Illinois. They were the parents of Edith May, Margaret Sarah, and David Edwin John.

Jenet John married Almond Jose in Grass Valley, Nevada. Their children were Richard Henry, Mary Elizabeth, John Lloyd, Al (who died shortly after birth), Thomas, Margarite, and Jenny Jose.

Sophia John married David Clement. They had a son, David, and a baby boy who died even before he was given a name.

Thomas John married Lala Kift from Stratford-on-Avon. Lala's mother, Susana Brown, was related to the Duke of Kent. Thomas and Lala John had six children: Georgina, Dorothy, Melba, Lallie Jean, Thomas Samuel, and Eve Margaret.

With her husband, William, Margaret John Davis's family in Butte had grown to four children: Syl, Hattie, Will, and a baby, Florence.

One of the most cherished holidays for this large Welsh brood was March 1, St. David's Day, also called Eisteddfod, which came to be one of little Hattie's favorite celebrations because it meant food and fun and contests for singing and reciting in Welsh.

Hattie loved to read and spent all her free time reading poetry. Free time was precious because the women and the girls spent most of their time cleaning the soot from the smelter off the furniture and floors.

Hattie and most of the Welsh families attended the Welsh Presbyterian Church on the corner of Dakota and Aluminum Streets. "Services were in English and Welsh, and after Sunday School the Welsh language was taught to youngsters."[1] With her friends at the church, Margaret Davis spoke of the gently rolling hills of Wales and the fresh air from the Bristol Channel. The families missed the lunches of cockles, and laverbread, and meaty Welsh bacon. She spoke less lovingly of the dust in Butte, where the soot dimmed even close vision on the street. Margaret knew, however, that the dirt meant jobs, and no one could complain about that.

"Things were far different from the old times in Wales when the English would beat the Welsh school children for writing Welsh on the slates instead of the required English. A slab of wood with the words 'Welsh Not' carved into it was handed to the first pupil caught speaking Welsh on any day, and that pupil had to inform on any other offenders. They were all lined up at the end of the day and beaten with a cane."[2]

As St. David's Day arrived, Hattie ran to greet her friends as they came through the vestibule. She wore her favorite dress with the small handmade lace collar. Her blue ribbon looked light for early March, but this was her favorite celebration. Her mother told her to change earlier that morning, but Hattie answered that this was the special dress made by her. How could Margaret tell her no?

There were wonderful treats at Eisteddfod. There would be the *bara brith* and *ffagod*, and Welsh rarebit. "The Welsh choir would sing, 'March of the Men of Harlech.'"[3]

There were young boys at "St. David's Fest," as the boys called it. Their Welsh names made Hattie feel comfortable. Bernard was a gentle boy who enjoyed poetry. Gareth liked to sing in his quartet, and Vernon liked to

DESTINATION: BUTTE, MONTANA

WILLIAM DAVIS, DAUGHTER ADELINE (HATTIE) DAVIS, MARGARET JOHN DAVIS,
BABY IS FLORENCE DAVIS, AND MARGARET'S SISTER, SOPHIA JOHN

watch Hattie recite her poems. Some of the older Welsh wore the sprig of leek, the symbol of Wales. It was flattering to receive so much attention as she swirled around the vestibule.

Hattie loved Welsh poetry. She was clever enough to recite the complex rhythms. She liked the sound of the *cynghanedd* (sound chiming). She was modern enough to enjoy the *pryddest* (free verse). Hattie hoped to win first place; she would cherish the ribbon.

When it was her turn to compete, Hattie entered the church, and the door of the vestibule closed behind her. The interior was not too large. The windows began at her waist and reached almost twenty feet to the ceiling. The black wrought iron grates on the floor circulated the heat, making the church warm and cozy. March was still very cold in Butte. The waxed floors shone almost enough to see her reflection.

After looking quickly at the judges, Hattie began her recitation in Welsh. The judges looked on approvingly, and although they didn't comment or smile broadly, she knew she performed well.

JOHN DANIEL CLANCY ARRIVES IN BUTTE, MONTANA

D anny's mother and father had traced the two branches of the family tree with long stories. He could hear his father's voice telling the tale of John D. Clancy's arrival in Butte.

John D. Clancy came from Claddagh village, County Galway, Ireland. John D. was a hard worker, and had a quick wit and self-deprecating sense of humor. He also had many stories about Claddagh village, a cluster of thatch-roofed cottages on Galway Bay, separated from Galway City by the rushing waters of the River Corrib. The Claddagh ring originated there—showing two hands touching one heart. It was said a Dominican priest started feeding swans in Galway Bay, and when others spread their wings to migrate, seventy-five of the birds continued to float in the bay, reluctant to leave.

Following the famine in 1847, those in Galway struggled and could not recover financially. The Claddagh fishing fleet of "hookers," as they were called, suffered greatly. Some in charge thought the barefoot poor could somehow pay rent on the small cottages, so if no rent were paid, all belongings were placed in the street.

Later there were Galway hosiery and clay pipe factories, but they came too late for John D.'s employment. After his mother's slow death from a lung ailment, he was determined to try his luck across the sea. He had no brothers or sisters, so it was not difficult to set sail for America. He made his way to Utah in 1870 and found work at a silver mine. After a time, John D. left Utah for the Butte mines, where many of the Irish immigrants came from Galway. Copper baron Marcus Daly had let it be known in Ireland that he would put any Irishman to work in Butte. John D. thought "three and one-half dollars a day"[1] was great pay. He loved the sights and sounds of Butte. He loved the politics as well. In Ireland they were life or death; here they were more of a game.

John D. reflected on the men of power in Butte. William A. Clark, better known as W. A. Clark, was the first of the Copper Kings to arrive in the ore-laden city. As an American of Irish descent, W. A. had been a schoolteacher before establishing some mining claims in the Bannack gold strike. He decided to make quick money selling food and supplies to miners. Clark then worked in mining in Deer Lodge, Montana, in 1863. "He married Kate L. Stauffer, a childhood sweetheart … from Pennsylvania."[2]

He arrived in Butte just as placer mining there died out, but he knew mining and recognized the area's possibilities. He bought the Colusa, the Original, the Gambetta, and the Mountain Chief mines. Then Clark left Butte to attend the Columbia School of Mines. When he returned, he quickly built his fortune.

Clark treated his workers well. He was responsible for the eight-hour workday. Every Clark employee looked forward to a Christmas turkey. He developed the Columbia Gardens for his miners, knowing he would lose money on the operations of the gardens. W. A. Clark said, "The Columbia Gardens is my monument. Of my many business enterprises it is the one I love best, and it is practically the only one on which I lose money."[3]

The second Copper King, Marcus Daly (the first Copper King in John

D.'s mind), was a true hero to all Irishmen. One of eleven children from the Daly clan in rocky County Cavan, Ireland, Daly arrived in America in 1856 with only 50 cents in his pocket. He worked on the docks in New York City to earn the fare to San Francisco via Panama. He met Tom Murphy, and the two of them traveled to mines in northern California. Daly was determined to make a career of mining. Daly worked in the Comstock Mine in Nevada, and earned the reputation of being an expert—as the man who could see inside of mountains. Later he worked for the Walker brothers in Utah and recommended they buy the Anaconda Copper Mine because it was rich in copper and silver. Marcus knew copper was going to be more valuable than gold because of the need for copper in telegraph lines and the development of electricity for power and lighting. He arrived in Butte in 1876, and when Daly bought Michael Hickey's mine, the Anaconda, people knew Daly was becoming a man of power.[4]

Daly was friendly to all his men. He knew many of them by name. John D. liked that. Daly also had a reputation for taking care of widows and children, annually donating 200 tons of coal to assist those unable to afford wood for heat during the cold winters. "Damn fine fellow, that Marcus!" was the toast as John D. raised a drink to him on payday.

John D. especially enjoyed the Butte Race Track owned by Daly. Daly loved horses and loved to bet on his horse, Tammany. The miners, too, had money to bet. "It was Daly's custom to give his miners the shift off—with pay—that they might attend the sport of kings."[5]

In 1893, W. A. Clark's and Marcus Daly's "war" escalated over politics. Clark ran for the U.S. Senate, but his bid for office stalled when Daly helped uncover bribes that Clark had paid for votes. The two Copper Kings then battled over which Montana city should become the seat of government. Butte backed Marcus Daly's attempt to place the Montana capital in Anaconda. W. A. Clark wanted Helena to be the site of the state capital. After the vote was taken, Helena received "27,028 votes over Anaconda with 25,118."[6] There were rumors of altered ballots, but most of the miners did not think the site of the capital was important to them.

Certificate of Naturalization

In the District Court of the Second Judicial District of the State of Montana

IN AND FOR THE COUNTY OF SILVER BOW

Hon. _William Clancy._ _Judge Presiding._

In the Matter of the Application of

John Clancy .... an Alien,
to become a Citizen of the United States of America.

In Open Court this _26th_

day of _Oct_ .....A. D. 189_8_

It Appearing to the Satisfaction of this Court, By the oaths of _Albert Hensley_ and _James Mackey_ ...., Citizens of the United States of America, first duly sworn and examined, that the above named applicant is a native of _Ireland_ .... has resided within the limits and under the jurisdiction of the United States for the five years last past, and in the State of Montana for the year last past; and that during all of said five years' time he has behaved as a man of good moral character, attached to the principles of the Constitution of the United States, and well disposed to the good order and happiness of the same.

And it also Appearing to the Court, By competent evidence, that the said applicant has heretofore, and more than two years since, and in due form of law, declared his intention to become a citizen of the United States of America, and having now, here, before this Court, taken the oath that he will support the Constitution of the United States of America, and that he doth absolutely and entirely renounce and abjure all allegiance and fidelity to every foreign Prince, Potentate, State or Sovereignty whatsoever, and particularly to .... VICTORIA, Queen of Great Britain and Ireland and Empress of India, of whom he has heretofore been a subject.

It is Therefore Ordered, Adjudged and Decreed, That the said _John Clancy_ be, and he is hereby admitted and declared to be a Citizen of the United States of America.

Signed _John Clancy_

Signed ...._Applicant._

Signed ...._Judge._

JOHN D. CLANCY'S NATURALIZATION CERTIFICATE

Although the Copper Kings were consumed by the mining business, they never forgot their workers and their families. W. A. Clark built and donated a children's home to the Associated Charities in memory of his son, Paul, who died in 1898 at sixteen years of age. W. A. Clark shared his memory of Paul, who from his earliest years gave all of his savings to the poor, especially for the Fresh Air Fund. John D. would read about it in the Butte *Daily Inter Mountain.*

"The project of the establishment of the home was inspired by the premature demise of a noble boy whose name it bears. A more unselfish child never lived than he. He kept a small bank, which he would empty from time to time and donate the contents to some charitable object." To raise funds for the new Paul Clark Home, the Associated Charities sponsored the Charity Ball on November 17, 1900. "W. A. began his 10:00 p.m. address at the Ball: 'It has been said that he who causes two blades of grass to grow where only one grew before, is a benefactor. What then shall be said of him or her, who allays the pangs of physical distress, brightens the tear-bedimmed eye, reclaims the fatherless or abandoned infant or directs the erring step of youth and innocence into pathways that lead to happiness or honor.'

"The Charity Ball drew a crowd of 1,500. Carriages continued to arrive after midnight. The receipts from the ball totaled $1,250.00. The completed price for the Paul Clark Home on the corner of Excelsior and Mercury Streets was $50,000.00.

"The 'piece de resistance' of the whole architectural scheme is what is termed the 'sun parlor,' which connects to the main rooms with the hospital. There were tropical bowers of nodding palm, snowy chrysanthemums, varied in multitudinous hues. The flowers had all been grown in the 'sun parlor.' J. H. Mitchell who tended the flowers at the Columbia Gardens was responsible for the wonderful effects."[7]

While Clark and Daly vied for public acceptance and built financial empires, a third Copper King found his way into the Butte panorama. Augustus Heinze arrived in Butte in 1889. He had been a student at the Columbia School of Mines, and later he worked for the Boston and Montana Consolidated Copper and Silver Mining Company for $5 per day.[8]

Heinze was of German descent; he was young and ambitious. He bent his elbow with the miners, and the women in Butte considered him an eligible bachelor.

John D. watched the developing war of the Copper Kings with incredible fascination. He loved politics and game playing. John D.'s many acquaintances included the staff at the W. A. Clark mansion on Granite Street. This was quite the place to behold for a simple miner. The thirty-four-room redbrick mansion was built from 1884 to 1888 for $250,000 on the largest lot on Granite Street. Inside were the finest furnishings. Outside were landscaping and ornate ironwork.

The Clark mansion, like a number of other houses in Butte, was fashioned after houses in New York City, according to reports of those who had been to New York. Every inch of the lot was utilized. Elaborate porches replaced a large lawn.

Similarly, the tall, stark boardinghouses in the simpler neighborhoods were so close together that the laundry hanging from one house would touch the next if any breeze blew at all.

Down past the central district was the Cabbage Patch. These hastily built cabins were miner's homes. Farther down on Mercury Street was Venus Alley, where girls behind windows tapped on the panes, luring potential customers to sample their charms.

CHAPTER 6

POLITICS AND LIFE AS A MINER

E ventually, John Daniel worked for Marcus Daly in the Mountain Consolidated, known as the Mountain Con. John loved the bustle of Butte, and he liked earning a good living. At that time, the employees numbered 6,548 and the monthly payroll hit $1,000,000.[1] Down in the hole, the men worked hard, but they paced themselves. John stripped off his shirt and descended down in the cage with five others. It was blazing hot in the mines. His favorite shift was from 3 p.m. to 11 p.m. He would come off shift and stop at one of more than 200 bars for a Shawn O'Farrell—a shot of whiskey and a beer. The cold foam was such a welcome sensation after leaving the sweltering dungeon below.

John D. stepped into the cage next to Jim O'Toole. Jim nodded. There wasn't any way to converse once the cage settled below. It was a long and lonesome shift. A stub of a candle gave enough light for delicate pick work. John was anxious to end this shift and cool off with ice before going to the top.

The smoke in the air outside was so thick those nights that

there were loud clanging bells attached to the mule teams to avoid anyone being run over. John D. stopped at the Comique. In the center of a table were chips and cards. The players were serious; even those watching had serious expressions. John D. glanced around and saw the screened boxes where some of Butte's famous were watching the action, but preferred not to be seen. Entry had been made from the alley. "Each box entered from a narrow corridor invisible from the house, was provided with a bolt on the inside of its slide-through door through which trays of drinks or iced buckets of champagne could be passed."[2]

Many of the regulars, some bleary-eyed, sat on stools. The floors weren't clean, but the tables were immaculate. With round-the-clock drinking, it was impossible to scour the floor. Young boys ran beer to homebound customers who needed a beer by 10:30 p.m. After he downed a few, John D. went to his room at the boardinghouse and slept, and the next day and the next day were as before.

After years of this daily grind, it all abruptly changed. John Daniel Clancy met and then quickly married a widow, Ellen Casey Newman. Ellen had one daughter, Eileen, and three sons: Thomas, Patrick, and Johnny. Within a year, John and Ellen were the parents of a son, Daniel John Clancy.

MAYBELLE HOGAN
COUNTY SUPERINTENDENT OF SCHOOLS
OF SILVER BOW COUNTY
BUTTE, MONTANA

May 21, 1942

TO WHOM IT MAY CONCERN:

According to the Census Records (of Book 1892) kept in this office, Dan Clancy, son of Helen and John Clancy, who resided in the 800 Block on East Park Street in Butte, Montana, Silver Bow County, was born November 3, 1885.

Very truly,

Maybelle Hogan
Co. Supt. of Schools

VERIFICATION OF DANIEL JOHN CLANCY'S BIRTH CERTIFICATE

By this time, Augustus Heinze was in the midst of his greatest battle. John D. and all of Butte eagerly waited for the newspapers to hit the streets with the news of the Apex Trials. The trials focused on Heinze and the Anaconda Company. With thirty-seven attorneys on his staff, Heinze challenged the Company as it had never been challenged before.

John D. admired Heinze's quick mind. Heinze had made duplicate maps of what he learned when surveying for Boston and Montana. Heinze's case revolved around the source of the vein—the so-called apex law that gave mineral rights to whomever owned the surface of a vein, no matter where that vein led below ground. Heinze raised money back East and used his inheritance of $50,000 from his family in Germany[3] to build a smelter in Butte, which cut operating costs in half.

Heinze owned mining properties, including the Rarus Mine, but the Boston Company owned by Amalgamated was intent upon owning as much of the Butte copper properties as possible. Fearlessly, Heinze argued that his Rarus Mine's ore bodies apexed the Michael Davitt ore. The Boston Company countered that, under the apex law, the Boston Company owned the ore.[4]

While underground eating lunch one day, the men made bets on the Apex Trial. Seamus Dolan and John Daniel were the first to wager a bet. Seamus bet on the Company winning, but John bet on Heinze and the influence of Judge Clancy.

"Listen Seamus, Judge Clancy is no relative of mine," said John Daniel. "Did you see the head on that man? His wild eyebrows, his beard with the breakfast still in there? Did you ever see me with a chaw of tobacco? You'd never see Judge Clancy without a chaw even on the bench."

"On the bench," it was said in Butte, "Clancy was a burlesque of judicial dignity, but he was no joke."[5]

Seamus thought otherwise. "How can that crook, Judge Clancy, beat the Company lawyers? I'll bet you a day's wage the Company wins."

John D. liked to go to the courtroom and watch the trial before his shift in the mine. The courtroom was crowded for the first few days, but after the opening in court, most of Butte relied on the newspaper accounts.

John D. found a seat and eagerly watched—concerned because a day's wage bet was a considerable sum.

Even Wall Street eagerly watched the fights. Hundreds of lawsuits were pending. Ordinary lawsuits had to wait years.

Skilled mining surveyors and geologists identified mines, veins, and title. John was amazed that Heinze's own newspaper, *The Reveille,* was able to counter the forty-one newspapers supporting the Anaconda Company.

After months of legal battles, the Anaconda Company was beyond frustration. Their lawyers had always been feared, but in Judge Clancy's courtroom they were scorned. Judge Clancy issued a permanent injunction in October 1903. In turn, the Company asked the governor to call a special session of the legislature to consider a law that would allow for the disqualification of judges. When the governor refused, the Company ordered all of its mines, mills, and smelters of their subsidiary companies to shut down at once. Three thousand miners were immediately out of work.

Senator W. A. Clark, speaking for the Anaconda Company, told the hungry crowd that the cold, bitter winter was caused by Augustus Heinze.

Heinze was in a tight spot. He sent out word that he would make his statement on the steps of the courthouse at 4 p.m. Men and boys carried wooden boxes and vegetable barrels and piled them high at the foot of Utah Avenue. They set a bonfire to bring people to the rally.

When Heinze approached the steps, 10,000 people stood waiting to hear him speak. The Amalgamated officials were actually smiling for the first time in months.

For one and a half hours, Heinze spoke to the mob. There were people on the balcony behind him, on the same level in front of him, and to the left and to the right as far as he could see. He concluded the speech with these words: "My fight against Standard Oil is your fight—we stand or fall together—If they crush me tomorrow, they will crush you the day following. They will cut your wages and raise the tariff in the company store on every bite you eat and every rag you wear. They will force you to dwell in Standard Oil houses while you live, and you must be buried in Standard Oil coffins when you die. . . . Let them win tomorrow and they will inaugurate conditions in Montana that will blast its fairest prospect and make its very name hateful to those who love liberty."

"Napoleon! Napoleon!"[6] The crowd shouted in a frenzy.

DESTINATION: BUTTE, MONTANA

Heinze then set forth demands: They would sell shares at the price they had paid, provided that H. H. Rogers, the president of Amalgamated and a fellow attorney, and William Scallon, another attorney, pledge that the mines would be kept in continuous operation for a year and present wages would be maintained for three years.[7]

"William Scallon, resident director of the Amalgamated in Montana, proceeded to answer Heinze's specious offers and arguments, the affected miners were cold enough to give heed. With the convincing logic of an able lawyer, Scallon dissected and analyzed each detail of Heinze's emotional appeal."[8]

Scallon said the Amalgamated costs noted by Heinze far exceeded the total stated by Heinze. The issue of the right to the Nipper Mine would then allow Heinze a large part of ore rights to the Parrott and the Neversweat Mines, which could not be agreed upon. Scallon did acquiesce to Heinze's demand that the mines would be kept in operation and wages maintained: "neither Mr. Rogers nor myself would stand for any cut in wages."[9]

Finally, the War of the Copper Kings ended when the legislature convened and passed the law the Company requested, known as the Fair Trial Practices Law, which grants an automatic change of venue for either party in a suit if there was suspected prejudice of a judge. Amalgamated was eager to move their cases from Augustus Heinze and Judge Cloney's power.

CHAPTER 7 ⌘

DANIEL JOHN CLANCY AFTER HIS MOTHER'S DEATH

———————————————————————————— ⌘

The Clancy family enjoyed their life together until Ellen fell ill and died suddenly. John D. was still mining, but after the Heinze case ended, John found work with independent mining companies. His search for work made it difficult to take care of Daniel John. Daniel's much older stepbrothers were moving around prospecting, and his stepsister, Eileen, had moved to California, so for the time being John D. sent Daniel John to St. Joseph's Catholic orphanage in Helena, Montana. Six boys shared his room at the orphanage. Daniel felt terribly lonely there; he missed his mother, his stepbrothers, his stepsister, and his father. Although there were some orphans living at the home, most of the children came from families who could not afford to feed them.

St. Joseph's was at the end of Montana Avenue in Helena, well out of town. It was huge compared to the Clancy apartment in Butte. The floors were made of wood and were pol-

JOHN D. CLANCY AND DANIEL, HIS FIFTEEN-YEAR-OLD MINER SON

ished to a bright shine. Daniel soon discovered that the residents kept the floors in that condition. All of the children had many chores. If the floor didn't shine, the boys or girls assigned to that chore had to do it over and over again and sometimes many times until it gleamed. There were pens for animals in the back of the one-acre lot. Some of the younger children thought these pigs, cows, and rabbits were pets, but Daniel knew better. The orphanage was a massive brick building that was either freezing or too hot from the steamy, hissing radiators. After recess, the boys and girls came back inside with frozen socks that were damp for the rest of the day, until they went back outside and the socks froze again.

Daniel desperately wanted to be with his father, so after two runaway attempts, John took him back to Butte.

"Well, what shall I do with you?" pondered John D. "I do have a position in the mine, and the price of copper is good, but don't you want to go to school?"

"I just missed Butte so much, Pa," answered Daniel. "I couldn't wait to see the Highlands. I could work in the mines."

"Don't you know I wished so much more for you?"

"We could live together in your apartment on West Copper," pleaded Daniel.

"So be it," sighed John D. "This is not what your mother wanted for you. Her boys are all in the mining business now."

"Thanks for not taking me back to the orphanage, Pa."

Daniel loved all the action on the streets. "Lemons was Butte's gray-headed messenger 'boy,' who, only thirty-six years of age at his death, had the appearance of at least sixty. For twenty-five years he had carried trays with his slow, shuffling gait referred to as the 'Lemon's stride.' ... Lemons was never known to talk or betray a trust, even though he could have told sensational stories."[1]

Old Fat Jack, a Civil War veteran, sat outside the courthouse with his hackney. Contrary to his nickname, Jack was long and lean, and his beard was always well trimmed. He was a big gambler, and did not seem to mind losing frequently. He was said to have "switched from faro to horse racing for this reason: 'You are just as sure of losing your money and the bookmakers don't egg you on. You lose it quicker on a horse race and you don't have the painful suspense of a possible win.'"[2] Jack was always immaculately groomed, and he would give rides anywhere in Butte to politicians or anyone who could pay the fare.

Daniel often passed the Joss House on Colorado Street. It was called the Big Dog Joss House. The fragrance of burning incense crept onto the street. There were opium dens available for two bits or four bits. Customers would lie down in one of four bunks and inhale opium vapors from peanut oil lamps.

"The lottery tickets had eighty numbers printed in Chinese characters. Each player marked out with a writing brush certain of the characters usually ten to fifteen, depending on the price paid for the ticket. If enough of the characters marked out turned up in the drawing, the player won varying amounts … The drawings were held every fifteen minutes."[3]

HATTIE DAVIS AND OTHER EMPLOYEES OF THE PAUMIE DYE HOUSE
ENJOY THEIR PICNIC AT THE COLUMBIA GARDENS (HATTIE IN THE BACK
ROW 3RD FROM LEFT NEXT TO HER FRIEND, SARA, 4TH FROM THE LEFT)

DESTINATION: BUTTE, MONTANA

PART III
CHAPTER 8 ✺

DANIEL CLANCY AND HATTIE DAVIS MEET

Years passed, and the John family lost their beloved Margret on July 3, 1906. As a farewell picnic, all of the Davises and Johns took a huge wagon to Elk Park. Most of the day was spent in traveling, but the cousins enjoyed being together. That sense of camaraderie soon came to an end at the reading of her will when it was learned that Margret had left her house to her daughter and son-in-law, Margaret and William Davis. Most of Margret's children contested the will and the matter eventually went to court. After that, most of the John offspring were estranged from the Davis family. Cousins born later did not realize they were related. Only Sophia remained close to Margaret and William and her nieces and nephews.

The years brought other changes as well. Hattie had grown into a modern woman earning a salary at the Paumie Parisian Dye House, which dated back to 1887 when Marie Paumie came to Butte from France. While heading to work one Tuesday, Hattie's life took a new turn. Daniel Clancy and Hattie walked past each other on Park Street. Daniel was taken with Hattie's delicate walk, slim build, and gentle smile. She did not have a robust laugh, but she appeared to have a quick sense of humor as she talked to the tall, strapping young man with her. Hattie noticed Daniel's rapt appraisal and blushed; she had few beaus. He noticed she carried books.

Two weeks later—again on a Tuesday—Daniel saw Hattie entering the library. For once, he was grateful for his Catholic school training and the nun's strict demands that he learn to read. Daniel followed Hattie and watched her browse in the poetry section. Daniel himself read Yeats and enjoyed Irish poetry.

Hattie had three books to check out. Daniel, who had been hovering nearby, gently bumped her arm, and the books started to fall. Hattie caught one, and Daniel caught the other two. He apologized for his clumsiness and asked how often she came to the library. Hattie said she checked out three books every other week and that poetry was her favorite.

Hattie was surprised that she talked so much to this stranger. Daniel reached out his hand and told her his name. She extended her fingers to touch his small, rough hand and told him her name and that she worked at the Paumie Dye House. Daniel asked if she would like to get a cup of coffee or tea, but Hattie said she was expected home with groceries for supper. She invited him to come to her home to meet the family.

Daniel said he would be happy to come sometime. But inwardly he worried that he would be on unequal footing meeting her family when he didn't have a family to greet her in return. His father, John D., was buried next to his mother, Ellen, and it had been years since Daniel had seen his stepbrothers and stepsister.

One week later, Hattie was again at the library. She hoped to see Daniel, but her careful choice of dress was for naught.

The next Sunday her mother, father, brothers, and sister took a picnic to the Columbia Gardens. Hattie thought W. A. Clark must be the grandest man ever to have built such a wonderful place. Hattie longed to go to the gardens with a beau and dance under the stars. There were dances every weekend in the summer, and the tri-level pavilion featured a dance hall and a restaurant that could serve 400 people.

As she daydreamed, Hattie basked in the cool shade under the spreading "branches of Canadian and balsam poplars, also known as Balm of Gilead."[1] It was like being transported to another country. There were countless flowers, and the red benches were comfortable to sit on and relax.

Hattie's baby brother, Thomas, was trying to crawl to the beautiful five-foot butterfly landscaped from yellow and brown pansies. Everything was carefully groomed and the grounds were immaculate. What a contrast to most of Butte, where there was barely a patch of ground for a yard.

Hattie, Syl, and Will ran toward the roller coaster. Hattie loved the tangled emotions at the start of the ride. You climbed slowly, slowly, and almost stopped, and then your breath was pushed back inside as the roller coaster flew. The rails were so smooth they never squeaked. Will let out a huge roar as the roller coaster sailed along. Down below, a head turned at the sound.

"That was the young man who was with Hattie on Park Street," thought Daniel.

Just as the roller coaster glided to an abrupt stop, Hattie saw Daniel. She gave a delicate wave and smiled. Daniel took one look at her possessive brothers and sucked in a fast breath. He walked over and extended his hand to Will. Will introduced himself, and introduced the quiet Syl, as well. Hattie asked Daniel to join their family for their picnic.

Margaret and William Davis were quiet, well-mannered people. Daniel was grateful that the younger sister, Florence, and the baby, Thomas, were diverting attention away from him.

Comfortable with their infrequent conversation, Daniel sat down and took a few sips of tea. Margaret's picnic was carefully unpacked from the hamper basket. A cloth was spread over a picnic table and Hattie helped to pass the dishes and utensils.

Daniel could not remember ever seeing such delicate food. Even wine glasses were on the table. He complimented Margaret on the lovely picnic even though he preferred the plainer Irish pasties to these "Cousin Jack" pasties with the carrots.

Will challenged Daniel to race to the pavilion. Daniel raised his right eyebrow, smiled his one-sided grin, and took off. Daniel beat Will in half the time.

"What a fun family," Daniel thought as he waved good-bye to the Davises as they boarded the trolley for home. He preferred to take a later trolley by himself.

The next day was Tuesday, and Daniel was sitting in the library when Hattie entered. He told her he was glad to see her. He wanted a book on mining; he thought he had an idea to improve the lighting in the mines. Daniel was a bit uncomfortable when he told Hattie he had never checked out a library book, but she was so matter-of-fact that she put him at ease. Hattie invited Daniel to Sunday dinner, and when he smiled and promised to come, she gave him directions to the Davises' home.

CHAPTER 9 ✎

THE MEN UNDERGROUND

The next day on his shift in the mine, Daniel gave a wave to Jim Dolan and Matt Welsh as they stood in the cage. The cage was attached to a cable that hung from a tall, metal headframe over the mine shaft. The cages held six men and were stacked on top of each other. Six men could ascend or descend in a single cage. The headframes seemed to reach to the sky when Daniel looked up from inside the cage. In Butte, the steel giants were called gallows, or gallus frames.

Daniel, Jim, and Matt were working a vein with heavy sledgehammers, a chore they called double jacking. They hammered the drills into the rock to prepare blasting holes. As the three crawled into the vein, Daniel passed Nellie, the mule, and gave her a pat. There were 1,000 mules working in the mines.

"How's she goin, Nell?" said Daniel as he sang the Old Miner's Ballad:

"My sweetheart's a mule in the mine.
I drive her with only one line.

On the dashboard I sit
And tobacco I spit,
All over my sweetheart's behind"[1]

The funny song was not the only reason Daniel was smiling. He was thinking of his upcoming Sunday dinner with Hattie.

Jim was tamping the round to blast. They were on the first shift, but at times the shifts overlapped. They drilled forty-five holes, each nine feet deep, into the face of the drift (like a tunnel). If one shift worked faster, everyone had to pick up the pace. If not, the next shift had to catch up and move on. The first shift drilled, the second shift blasted, and the third shift mucked out the blast debris. If it worked perfectly, the men would clear two "rounds"—piles of ore—in twenty-four hours.

After drilling the holes, the men would tamp in the dynamite with a wooden stick. It was a clear cut, and Matt moved the candle closer for accurate position of the holes. The drilled holes were loaded with dynamite and Jim tamped them in place with a wooden tool. The dynamite had to go off in sequence, with the bottom holes going off first. Daniel yelled, "blast your lifters!" The idea was to cut the fuse by hand, getting the length just right. Setting fuses was a real art. Matt hated the headache from the nitroglycerin in the dynamite. Only the shot and a beer waiting at the end of his shift would obliterate it. The men tamped the explosive, lit the fuses, and retreated. The rumble could be felt thousands of feet above at the surface.

Daniel was not fond of the blasting. He preferred to shovel the high-grade ore into cars, and he didn't mind the timbering. The mines needed tremendous amounts of lumber for shafts and braces as the thousands of mine workings were driven farther underground.

The time until lunch seemed long. Daniel eagerly opened his graniteware bucket, pushing the long handle to the side. He had an Irish pasty packed by Maureen, the helper at his boardinghouse. There also was an apple and strong tea. The miners were anxious to end the shift. Daniel had three more days on this job, and then he would go shoveling ore for a week or two.

Matt, Jim, and Daniel entered the changing room after they came to the top. Their work clothes were hung neatly for the next day, an old rule of

MINERS INCLUDING DANIEL JOHN CLANCY (2ND ROW FROM THE BOTTOM, 4TH FROM LEFT)

Marcus Daly's that was still enforced. The large barrel-shaped stove in the center of the room almost warmed Daniel as he showered quickly and put on his change of clothes.

More than a few of the miners were tempted to help themselves to a lump of copper when they ended their shift, but Daniel was not one of them.

Daniel left the Mountain Con and walked over town. He thought a couple of cold beers and a game of faro might be enjoyable. Frank Sherwin, dealer at the M&M Bar, was shuffling the cards as the table filled with players.

Daniel looked around at the huge back bar. There were gleaming bottles of every kind of liquor. The cash register rang so often he almost couldn't hear the sounds of laughter and shouts from the gaming table in the back.

The bar was full. The tables were still more than half full. Even at midnight, Butte was roaring.

He walked to the faro table, not sure if he felt lucky or not. Stools were seats for the poker table, but faro was played at a regular table with comfortable chairs. The men wore their hats while they played. Daniel tried to determine the luckiest style of hat as men placed their bets on cards in the "layout," the full suit of spades laid on the table. He placed his own bet and then watched as Frank skillfully cut and shuffled a deck of cards. Frank set the deck face up in a wooden dealing box, discarded the top card, known as the "soda," and then pulled the next two cards from the box. Bets on the layout that matched the face value of the first card drawn were losing bets, and those that matched the second card were winners. Daniel thought the odds were much like roulette, and luck seemed to favor the dealer. Daniel and the other punters looked at the cards as Frank laid them on the table to see who had won. Daniel lost on the first turn. He frowned as Frank scooped up his few chips, and then he turned and left the table. It was Daniel's rule that if he didn't win right away, he was bound to be unlucky the rest of the night, and so it was prudent to quit.

CHAPTER 10

DAN AND HATTIE'S COURTSHIP

It was Sunday and the table was set for Hattie's beau. She picked pansies for the center of the table. Her brothers sat reading, noting her nervousness. Will kidded Hattie about resetting the table three times. Hattie reminded him that he was on pins the first time Clara, his girlfriend, came to dinner.

Margaret checked the house again and plumped up the pillows on the sofa. She gently placed the ribbon pillow on top.

Daniel knocked softly at the door. He had brought Hattie a box of hand-dipped chocolates from the American Candy Shop.

The Davis family enjoyed the dinner of Welsh caul, but Daniel didn't care for lamb. He hoped he ate enough, so Margaret wouldn't be offended.

The family sat in the living room after dinner and discussed working in the mines, who had the best foreman, and who was the best mine owner. Syl and Will both worked at the Leonard Mine. Daniel learned that Syl and Will usually worked together and preferred the dynamite work. The usually silent Syl said they liked the precision such dangerous work required.

HATTIE DAVIS

Hattie's father, William, was quiet all evening. After Daniel left, William motioned for Hattie to sit with him on the porch then asked why she was so taken with Daniel. Hattie smiled and said Daniel wasn't a braggart like many young men she knew. William was concerned because Daniel was almost too quiet and was so alone with no family. Hattie told her father that Daniel enjoyed being with their family.

After ten months of these family outings, Hattie and Daniel made plans to marry. There were some difficulties, beginning with the wedding ceremony. Daniel had not gone to church since Hattie met him, so the subject of religion had not been discussed. Hattie tried to remain calm despite the fact that her family had all of the wedding arrangements in place when Daniel told her they needed to marry and raise any children they would have in the Catholic Church. Hattie tried to explain how she and her family had been attending their Presbyterian church since her family arrived from Wales. All of their friends saw them there every week. It was an intrinsic part of their lives.

Daniel said he was sorry, but he was adamant. He couldn't marry her in the Welsh Presbyterian Church because he couldn't marry outside the Cath-

DANIEL CLANCY

olic Church. As he pulled away from her, Hattie gave in. She told him to call the priest and make the arrangements. Hattie's mother, Margaret, appraised the situation carefully. She did not approve of these new complications.

DANIEL AND HATTIE'S WEDDING AND EARLY MARRIED LIFE

The morning of the wedding, Hattie still felt nervous. She wore her mother's wedding gown, and the white silk and lace fit her perfectly. Margaret had embroidered the veil, which was held in place by delicate orange blossoms. Some of Hattie's friends chose gold or peach for their wedding gowns since those were the newly fashionable colors. However, Hattie preferred to carry on a family tradition in the beautiful gown that accentuated her waist and almost bared her shoulders in a way that gave her a fragile look.

Daniel wore a black suit. He looked immaculate. Syl and Will could not understand how a miner could have such clean hands.

Hattie felt a wave of sadness as she thought of her father. His death three months earlier had left the family in a quiet, reflective mood. In his absence, Syl and Will would walk their sister down the aisle. Florence was Hattie's maid of honor. Tommy was also excited to be part of the celebration.

Hattie felt overwhelmed by the size of Holy Cross, the Catholic Church, located not too far from her cozy little Welsh church. The priest seemed too reserved. The young bride fidgeted throughout the ceremony, trying to figure out when to stand, kneel, or sit. She gave a sigh of relief when the vows were said and it was time to leave.

Hattie was anxious to get to her own church for the reception. All of her friends were there. As soon as the newlyweds arrived at the Welsh church, Hattie walked over to hug Bess and Sara, who had worked with her at Paumie's and now looked so pretty in their dresses. They were both in love and planned to marry soon, so they thoroughly enjoyed this wedding spirit.

The soft music, dainty punch glasses, and the finger foods were foreign to the new bridegroom. Daniel tried to mix, but quiet receptions were not the rule at Irish weddings, where spirited revelry could go on for hours and sometimes days. Daniel was glad when it was time to leave the hall for the carriage ride to their apartment in the boardinghouse on Leatherwood Street. Daniel didn't have to work for two days. He wouldn't be paid, but he and Hattie needed time to be alone. He gently lifted Hattie and carried her over the threshold. Hattie was nervous as Daniel undid the tiny buttons on her dress. She fingered the slender gold ring as Daniel gently kissed her.

In the morning, Hattie awoke to the aroma of fresh coffee; it had never smelled so delicious. Hattie figured it must be the smallness of the apartment that allowed the smell to permeate the air. Daniel also prepared toast and brought the breakfast to Hattie. He was accustomed to early mornings from his time at St. Joseph's Orphanage. After breakfast, they walked over town. When they returned, there was a basket of goodies from Margaret for their dinner.

The next day Hattie cooked breakfast and washed one of Daniel's shirts. She hung the shirt and a few other pieces of laundry on the empty line outside.

Hattie loved to embroider or do any type of handwork. She helped her mother finish linens. Hattie planned to talk to Margaret about continuing this work, since her job at Paumie Dye House was over. Wives seldom worked in Butte—men were supposed to be the breadwinners for their families.

The following day, Daniel left for work at 3 p.m. Margaret asked Hattie if she would like to come over for the evening, but Hattie had some new books to read and she spent her first evening alone. The boardinghouse was not too hot in early June, and evenings always cooled quickly in Butte. There wasn't too much smoke that night, so she opened the window and welcomed the breeze.

She fixed tea for Daniel at midnight, but he didn't get home until 12:30. Hattie asked if he still wanted the tea, but he told her that his usual routine was to stop by the M&M for a beer after his shift.

The next year, their first child, Margaret Clancy, was born. She would be called Marg to avoid confusion with her grandmother's name. She was a sweet child, slept well, and seldom fussed. The baby needed to be baptized a Catholic, so Hattie sewed a christening gown with French knots and a smocked bodice. The gown was so beautiful, and brown-eyed Margaret was so dear—she looked like a doll wrapped in the pink quilted blanket made by her grandmother. Hattie's brothers bought a carriage for Marg.

Sophia often would visit Margaret Davis and her nieces and nephews. Sophia and her son, David Clement, lived on Park Street. Sophia's husband, Dave Clement, had left Butte to find better mining possibilities, but his letters became more and more infrequent, and finally, after two years, Sophia knew she was alone with her son. David, who was only fifteen, tried to support them by driving a milk wagon for the Holstein Ranch. One day, with the bottles of milk clanking loudly, he did not hear a rapidly approaching train as he crossed the tracks. He died on November 5.[1] Sophia could not bear the loss. She began to drink heavily and succumbed to her sadness four years later. She was buried next to her son in Mount Moriah Cemetery in Butte.

CHAPTER 12 ꙮ

THE YOUNG CLANCY FAMILY

Hattie continued to do sewing for women in Butte and soon found herself pregnant again. It was welcome news. She liked to make up stories as she and Marg sat in the early evenings. Hattie sipped tea and wove tales of Merlin, the magician, one of her favorite characters. Hattie thought fondly of Wales when they talked of Merlin. It was as though she had spent more than her time of birth in that country.

Hattie and Daniel looked for a house to buy. They had been saving money and it looked like they could afford a new bungalow on Hazel Street. Hattie especially loved the ginger-bread trim on the outside.

When moving time came, Daniel hugged her and told her not to lift anything heavy because he would take care of everything. Hattie couldn't wait to have more space for children. There was a small yard, and she quickly planted tall, gold marigolds.

A month later, Hattie's brother Will and his wife, Clara,

and their sons, Gordon and Billy, moved into a new house across the street. The next month, Syl and Rose and their three daughters, Rosemary, Joan, and Sylvia, moved into a bungalow two doors down from Will and Clara.

One baby, another baby coming, and now a new house. Daniel was amazed by all of the changes. His family had never owned a house. The young miner felt very proud.

Florence Davis enjoyed her niece and looked forward to helping with the new baby. When the baby arrived, Hattie spent one week in bed, then had another week to ease into the new routine.

The Clancys named this second daughter for Hattie's sister, Florence, calling her Flo. Both Marg and Flo favored the Davis side of the family. They had gentle temperaments, gentle smiles, and quiet laughs. Daniel himself had a subdued laugh, unlike many Irish who laughed heartily with eyes all a twinkle.

When little Marg asked Daniel to tell her stories, Daniel said he didn't know any stories. When Marg further asked if his mother hadn't told him stories, Daniel just said she hadn't known any stories either. It was difficult for Daniel to reflect at all on his mother, because of her early death. Marg didn't ask her Papa to tell stories after that. She would just pick out a book for him to read to her and to the baby, Flo.

As winter came on, Hattie watched neighbor women rustle coal. They would climb up the sides of coal cars idled on the railroad tracks and throw out pieces of coal, then collect them to burn in their stoves at home. There was poverty in Butte. In earlier times, Marcus Daly had provided free coal to help keep families warm.

A year passed as Daniel and Hattie expected a third child in the spring. Hattie loved the babies and their soft skin, and their darling, tiny fingers delighted her.

Daniel thought he would like a son. He had no relatives that he knew of. In Butte, the Clancy name belonged to the old judge, but Daniel had always been told they were not related. Even so, Syl and Will liked to tease him about his well-known "relative." Daniel knew, however, that he would be happy with another daughter. Marg and Flo hung on his every word. Finally, the baby girl arrived. She was named Dorothy.

CHAPTER 13 ᖶ

SCHOOL DAYS AND FAMILY LIFE

ᖶ

Marg left for school clinging to her Papa. Daniel squeezed the little hand in his, and told her she would be happy to be there after the first week of school. Marg softly whispered that she didn't know anyone. Her frightened downcast eyes tried to hold back the tears. Daniel tried to offer some comfort to her by reminding her that she already knew how to read.

Marg waved two fingers as her Papa slid out the door. Marg stared at the other children who looked equally scared. Miss Flynn, the teacher, put her hands on Marg's shoulders, smiled, and firmly directed her to a row of desks. She said a card bearing her name would mark Marg's desk.

There was a large stove in the middle of the room that took the chill off. The windows were tall and heavy and had to be held open with a book to clear away the smoke from the stove.

As she looked for her name card, Marg walked gingerly across the floor, hoping the wooden slats wouldn't squeak much. She couldn't wait to tell Flo, Dorothy, and her Mama and Papa all of the experiences when she got home!

With the help of Miss Flynn, everybody finally found his or her desk. Some children didn't know how to read their names. Others couldn't speak clear English. Marg felt sorry for them.

As Miss Flynn printed a few words on the large blackboard, Tommy O'Brien poked Marg and asked her if she knew how the teacher would use the long pointer. Marg knew it was to show words. Tommy said that it was for the teacher to jab at bad children. Marg's eyes narrowed as she viewed what now looked like a cruel instrument. Tommy then asked her if she knew what happened in the cloakroom. Marg shook her head and turned away; she knew they were expected to be quiet. Marg put her head on the desk; she didn't feel well. She would have asked to be excused to use the bathroom, but she didn't know where it was.

On this first day, school only lasted through the morning. When lunchtime finally arrived, Marg was thrilled to see her mother pop her head inside the door. She smiled all afternoon as she clung to Hattie.

In no time, Marg was one of the best students in the class. She also was one of the kindest students, and the teacher asked her to help students hang up their coats in the cloakroom where the hooks were all placed at the same height for everyone. Little Emily Swenson always thanked Marg because she couldn't put her coat on the hook even if she jumped.

The stove in the classroom heated the room quickly each day. At first, it felt wonderful, but by 11 a.m., the room was horribly hot. Two students wore strong-smelling asafetida bags on cords around their necks to keep away colds. The aroma of garlic in some of the lunches hung in the air. One day Tommy O'Brien threw a handful of black pepper in the stove. It was difficult to decide who was sneezing from a cold and who was sneezing from the pepper. It didn't really matter since everybody's eyes were watering.

Although Marg was quiet, her classmates appreciated her smiles of encouragement. She had learned to add numbers quickly but couldn't explain the process to her Chinese classmate, Li Chin.

Li said that his father owned a bank and was able to add numbers more quickly than Miss Flynn. Marg replied that Miss Flynn was the teacher, so how could Mr. Chin be faster? Li invited Marg to come with him to see his father's bank.

The next day after school Marg walked with Li to the bank. His father bowed, Marg tried to bow back, but didn't know how, so she smiled shyly. Li Chin recited one of their arithmetic problems, and his father did the problem on something Marg had never seen before. It was about twelve inches long with round balls on wire. Li's father moved the balls around quickly. He came up with the correct answer faster than Marg could figure it on her fingers behind her back.

Marg asked Li what the instrument was that his father was using. He said it was an abacus, a tool from ages past that allowed the Chinese banks to do their figures faster than any others did. Marg hurried home to tell her Mama, Papa, and sisters about her adventure.

Fall faded and the holidays were approaching. Daniel loved Christmas in the mines because all of the men brought something to share on Christmas Eve. When he was a bachelor, he had asked Maureen, the boarding-house cook, to include extra stirabout (Irish porridge). Now he loved to pass around Hattie's *bara brith*. Daniel's tongue had finally learned to savor the delicate flavor as he passed around the specialty.

Joe Simonich brought *povetica*, the Serbian specialty, a Serbian bread so loaded with walnuts, butter, and honey that it should have been called a cake. Arne Larson brought fish jerky and Finnish sausage, which he made by pounding the marrow of venison and then stuffing it in the entrails of deer or elk. Chris Castigone brought frijoles and tortillas.

The lunch break usually lasted a half hour, but on this special day, it extended to an hour. The men ate until they were stuffed, and then looked for a *laggin* to set up for a short nap.

That Christmas, Hattie worked to make the season special for all of the family. The three girls would each have a doll. Marg and Flo picked out the style they liked from the *Sears and Roebuck* catalogue. The catalogue had been handled so often, the corners were bent. The printed cloth panels were ordered months before. Hattie sewed sides together, stuffed the dolls, and then sewed the dresses and embroidered the doll's faces. Marg's doll had purple bows, Flo's doll had pink ties, and Dorothy's doll was a baby with yellow ribbons. Since Daniel loved to fish, Hattie bought him a strong fishing basket. Daniel bought Hattie a book of Shakespeare's sonnets.

Daniel stayed by the Christmas tree until the candles were all lit. It was a glorious holiday for them all.

FLORENCE AND MARGARET OUTSIDE THE CLANCY HOME

CHAPTER 14 ﹋

WELSH AND CHINESE CUSTOMS TOLD IN SCHOOL

Hattie could not believe how quickly the years had passed. Marg was now in the third grade. Children in her class could invite grandparents to share stories or customs from their ancestors. Marg invited her grandmother, Margaret Davis, to talk about Wales and King Arthur and the wonderful Merlin. Marg beamed as her grandmother kept the class enthralled with the story of the fight to lead Wales.

Margaret began by saying that "Britain was a magical place where Merlin, the famous magician, seemed to appear and then disappear just as quickly. There were rumors that Merlin was born of a British princess and a dark angel. The power to know the future came from his father.

"In those times, people were superstitious. They wanted a strong leader; but their current leader, Vortigen, was a cruel man. Vortigen had to leave England, and subsequently became leader of Wales. Vortigen hired workers to build his Welsh castle, but, surprisingly, every night the day's work mysteriously collapsed. Vortigen was furious, and wanted to understand what was happening.

"A messenger was sent to Merlin to see if he knew the answer. Merlin paced for a while, then looked up. He did not have good news for Vortigen. Merlin said there were two strong dragons at war under the tower. One dragon was red, symbolizing the British, and the other dragon was white, symbolizing the Saxons. As for Vortigen, Merlin said, he would be paid for his evil doing. His nephews would overthrow him, and after the reign of the new king, Uther, England would have its greatest king."

Marg could not hold back the correct name when Margaret asked the class if they knew the name of this king. Marg screamed out: "It's King Arthur, and he is buried in Wales!"

Then Li Chin stood up to introduce his father. Mr. Chin unfolded a newspaper article. It was clipped from *The Butte Miner*, August 30, 1881, and explained a Chinese burial ceremony. At first, the class fidgeted, because they had sat still so long for the story from Wales, but then Mr. Chin captured their attention.

"The body was taken from the residence of the deceased. The gilt-papered coffin was placed inside the elegant hearse and a procession started for the Chinese cemetery on the flats. Scores of friends and relatives clad in Chinese costumes, their queues dangling down their backs, walked solemnly behind the hearse wearing bright ribbons on their wrist. On top of the hearse, two relatives of the dead man sat, one tossing out bright colored paper to fool the devils. The idea being that the latter would mistake the paper for money, start picking it up, and give the spirit of Chin time to escape. The other relative tossed handfuls of round papers with holes in the center, the notion being that those devils that were not picking up the money would have to hop through the hole in each paper and thus not make any great progress in following the procession.

" … At the cemetery more scraps of paper were tossed into the grave and a taper was burned at the end of the grave to attract the devil's attention. Punks burned at the foot of the grave because fire attracts the devil and his crew of friends!

"When Satan and his gang of demons had theoretically assembled, a fine banquet was set for them at the side of the grave, consisting of roast pork and chicken, boiled rice, apple dumplings, and other delicacies along with several bottles of rice wine and other imported Chinese liquors as an offering and bribe to Satan for permitting Chin's spirit to escape to the 'happy land.'

"The dead man's personal effects were burned in a bonfire, after which the body was lowered into the grave amidst much wailing and chanting, while the devil and his gang were busy eating the repast spread out for them.

"A Chinese priest murmured a prayer and threw the first shovel of dirt, while the mourners shook hands over the grave. Chinese candy and sweetmeats were then passed around the grave. A bit of China sugar and a dime, wrapped in paper, were given to every person present. The Chinese then solemnly took their departure leaving Chin to his ancestors. A number of white residents followed the procession ... and helped the devils to dispose of liquor and foodstuffs."[1]

The children were fascinated by this story. Those who were not Chinese were especially curious about what Satan was doing at a burial.

PART IV
CHAPTER 15 ♪

A CHANGED BUTTE

M arg, Flo, and Dorothy had been told by their parents to avoid certain neighborhoods as they walked around town. Many changes had occurred since the days when Hattie and Daniel walked about.

One day the children returned from the bakery and told their mother about curious-looking people eating mints on the street corners. Kept busy tending hearth and home, Hattie seldom went out and about. Until the children returned home with their story, she had no idea of what had been happening in her town.

Margaret, who was more world wise than her daughter, told Hattie that there were regular customers who picked up the prepackaged morphine at the local drug store, so store owners could make between $500 and $600 a month. There also were "Snowbirds,"[1] cocaine fiends who put the drug on the back of their hands and sniffed it up their noses. Hattie wondered how this could happen in Butte. It had never been a town of strict morality, but such an open use of narcotics was a shock. Hattie asked if anything was done to help these people.

Margaret said it didn't appear they wanted help. As for the mysterious mints the children had mentioned, Margaret said they were wafers of morphine. She added that their church had sent people out to help the addicts, but most were too far gone.

Margaret said it wasn't so easy to tell who was an addict—at least at first. The pastor said addicts might appear extremely nervous or excitable. In time, though, the evidence could be seen in their sunken eyes. Margaret said that Jere Murphy, the chief of police, said, "prowling the city, he often spotted men—and women too—that he knew he didn't want in Our Village."[2]

At bedtime that night, Hattie drew the children very close to her. She wished she could shield them from all the evils out there.

The next day, while Marg and Flo were in school, Hattie placed Dorothy in her buggy and they walked over town. Hattie was startled to see a motorized car turning on Mercury Street up from Main. The driver was dressed in a waterproof coat and wore a cap and goggles. The female passenger was wearing a silk coat and on her head was an adjustable straw hat. Over the ostrich plumes, there was a net. Hattie looked around for Fat Jack, remembering his query, "a carriage uptown?"

Elliott, the man at the wheel of this motorized car, was more accustomed to driving horses. The automobile lurched forward, and Elliott had a strange look in his eyes. He was grasping the wheel firmly, actually too firmly. Hattie heard him scream, "Whoa! Whoa! Damn you! Whoa!" The car ran into a telegraph pole a few feet beyond, and when Elliott was rescued, unhurt, he smiled apologetically, as he said, "I forgot I was not driving the grays."[3]

Later that day as Hattie walked toward Margaret's house, two men on the street corner laughed uproariously about the driver who forgot he wasn't driving a horse and couldn't make the taxi stop. Hattie knew Butte was in for incredible changes.

Priests, minister, pastors, and concerned citizens were all determined to clean up Butte's tarnished image. However, their efforts were stymied at every turn. When they boarded up the houses of prostitution on Mercury Street, the action moved to the back alleys. Sidewalks and lights led the way to the back of houses. Slumming parties were popular with the "exclusives" of town. Fat Jack drove carriages to the cheap entertainment. Men and women would line up for drinks at the bar. After the drinks were downed, they would all dance. The party went on for hours and only the heartiest would be standing by the end of the evening.[4]

"DOPE" VICTIMS ON INCREASE IN BUTTE

County Officers Suggest Establishment of Separate Quarters for Unfortunates at the Poorfarm.

THE HEADLINE IN *THE BUTTE MINER* ATTESTS TO THE 500 DRUG ADDICTS IN BUTTE

CHAPTER 16 ♫

THE NEW UNION AND WORLD WAR I

———————————————————— ♫

Butte's countless bars always had the twenty pieces on hand to cash the miner's checks. As time passed, however, many wives started to meet their husbands at the gates on payday so the checks would make it home.

The unions were vocal, and Daniel felt some of the men were becoming too violent. There no longer were any stories about Clark, Daly, or Heinze. A new breed of miners and mine owners had taken over.

In the late 1880s, in a mine with thirty employees, only two were still on the Butte hill at the end of a year. Now the names of workers were very familiar, since most miners had families to support and some of the men lived long enough to retire.

One evening Daniel received a telegram from his stepbrother, Johnny Newman. The telegram was an excited blur of words. Daniel picked up Hattie and swung her around. They were going to be rich! Johnny had struck silver in Nevada. He would send more details soon. The possibilities seemed endless. Daniel and Hattie waited and waited. Johnny never wrote again.[1]

Life went on. Hattie's sister, Florence, was working at the Town Talk Bakery in Meaderville. Florence loved Italian food and the closeness of Italian families, so it was only natural she was dating a young Italian, Charlie.

By 1914, many of the Welsh families were caught up in World War I. Both Syl and Will wanted to return to Wales to enlist, a common practice among Welshmen. Theirs was always a country of warriors. Legends told of red-haired men who were almost impossible to defeat.

A letter with news about the war arrived from their old friends, the Evanses. There was mention of nerve gas, which worried people in both Wales and in Butte. In an attempt to add some humor to the grim news, Gareth Evans asked Syl and Will how obituaries could be written if the Lion Pub in Llanymynech were hit. The pub straddled the border between England and Wales, as did a cemetery. "There are people buried in a local churchyard, with their heads in Wales and their feet in England."[2]

Butte sent many men to fight in World War I. Syl and Will planned to enlist, but Daniel did not. He was younger than Syl, but older than Will. Of the three, he looked oldest by far and was sick on and off with "the con," the miner's cough. Whenever he looked in a mirror, Daniel noticed he looked worn out. He thought he looked like the older miners he met when he first started mining. No matter whether his night had been fitful or restful, the same grayish skin tone and dark circles were always there.

When his friends, Arne Hansen and Filmore Larson, asked him to join them for a sauna, Daniel hoped it might be a healthy experience. That night, after a couple of drinks, the three men went to the Isam Sauna on Broadway. Daniel felt invigorated by the steam but could not bring himself to jump into the cold water afterwards. Both Arne and Filmore whipped themselves with the bundles of evergreens, as was the custom for the Finns.

Arne and Filmore worked together in the mines as partners. They explained to Daniel that Finns preferred that. The two men declined Daniel's offer to buy them a drink when they finished with the brisk dunk in the tub. Arne said his wife knew exactly how long it took to steam and to freeze and she expected him home after that. Daniel thought Hattie's gentle manner was more appealing than that of the demanding Mrs. Hansen.

Daniel continued to feel agitated because the unions were becoming difficult. There were arguments both in the mines and around the city. In 1914, martial law was declared. *The Butte Miner's* front page headlines read, "Disorders Mark the Celebration of Miners' Union Day," "Parade of Miners Is Broken Up by Insurgents and Headquarters of W. F. of M. Organization Wrecked and Records Destroyed," and "Alderman Is Thrown from Second Story."

Daniel tried to avoid confrontation. He would reword questions that seemed argumentative.

During the first week of June in 1914, the Old Miner's Union Hall was blown up. Miners from the American Federation of Labor withdrew from the union in protest against heavy assessments for benefits to striking miners in Michigan. They organized an Independent Miner Worker's Union.[3]

"On the night of June 12, the committee, six of 'em, was at the Spec, and expecting trouble. . . . They had called up Sheriff Tim Driscoll. . . . The miners disbanded and came downtown for a meeting at the auditorium." Muckey was there, and a young man named O'Brien, who could speak seven languages. He translated the proceedings to the crowd.[4]

The next day, the Miners' Union Day Celebration began with the traditional parade. The union officials were riding beautiful horses. The group marched down Main Street to Park and then progressed west. When the parade reached Dakota by Symon's Store and approached Sam Treloar's band, a mob burst upon the officials and pulled them off their horses.

The horses stomped into the crowd. A bottle hit the chief of police, Jere Murphy. The parade broke up, and there were mobs milling around town for hours.

"A cry rang out: 'To the Miner's Union Hall—tear it to hell and get the records! Wreck the house of the grafters.'"[5]

At the hall, typewriters, cash registers—anything that could be thrown—were smashed through the windows. In one hour, everything had been tossed into the street.

Frank Curran, acting mayor, begged the crowd to break up. "Somebody in the hall pushed him out of the window, and he fell to the street on top of a pile of carpet. His arm was broke [*sic*] and his ankle dislocated."[6] To calm the crowd and to get them to go home, the chief of police closed the saloons.

The police stayed away to prevent further bloodshed.

There were two union safes in the hall. The smaller of the two opened easily and was then thrown into the street. The larger safe would not open with sledges or chisels. The police came to retrieve the safe, and brought a large horse to cart it to City Hall. But the mob seized the horse and took the safe to Butte Reduction Works, where they planned to blow it up.

"Out stepped a lad from the crowd with a big bottle of some white looking stuff. 'This is nitro,' he says. 'I'm an old time safecracker. I'll show you how to open her.'

" … He poured the bottle into the cracks of the safe, put in a piece of fuse, and lit it with a match. The crowd backed away to safety. A bright blue flame came out of the cracks of the safe. The stuff was alcohol and the mob chased the would-be safecracker to hell away."[7]

Someone brought sticks of dynamite. After four blasts, it opened, and "$1,013 in one-dollar bills" were found. The money was given to one of the members for safekeeping. The mob headed back to town, but they couldn't get anything to drink, since Jere Murphy had closed everything down.[8]

The next day, the miners demanded that the five men arrested the day before be turned loose. City firefighters attempted to break up the crowd, but the crowd cut the hoses. To avoid further conflict, the five arrested men were set free.[9]

On June 21, Charlie Moyer, president of the Western Federation of Miners, came to town to patch things up. He asked the former officers to resign, and he planned to organize a new election.

". . . June 21, about four thousand miners met at the old Holland skating rink near the edge of Butte and organized a new Union. They elected Muckey McDonald president. Moyer came out in the papers declarin' that Western Federation wouldn't break up and called a meeting of that Union at what was left of its own hall for the evening of June 23.

". . . Moyer and about a hundred or so of the old Union men were in the hall. Moyer was making a speech. A few thousand had gathered out in front of the hall . . . . That stretch of the street had earned its nickname of 'Dardanelles.' Guns were in every window of the Union Hall—and they weren't cap guns. Smack into that crowd of miners gathered in front the bullets whizzed.

"One bunch went to the West Stewart Mine, half a block away, and made the engineers lower four men down into the mine to get the dynamite."[10]

The red building shook as thirty clicks were lit close to its edge. Again and again the blasts were set, but still the building stood. People in town had ridden all the way to the Columbia Gardens to be safe.

For the entire evening, every window in town shook, but only one wall came down in the Miner's Union Hall.

Although Hattie sensed the tension, Daniel didn't discuss union problems with her.

MINERS IN THE PARADE

—Photo by M. J. King.

The miners who were in the procession. Picture taken as the parade was proceeding north on Main street.

THE BUTTE MINER'S UNION DAY PARADE ENDS IN VIOLENCE

CHAPTER 17 ♪

FIRE AT THE SPECULATOR MINE

N early three years had passed since the union troubles, but there were troubles with World War I and senti-ment in Butte. The Columbia Gardens seemed like a perfect escape from the troubled times. It was a Friday, the 8th of June. Daniel was pleased that Hattie had planned the out-ing. Hattie, the girls, and Daniel rode the trolley to the gardens, carrying their picnic lunch and tableware. Daniel smiled at the other riders on the trolley, which was filled, with every pole supporting at least one person, all looking forward to relaxing at the gardens on this warm summer day. Marg and her friends walked up and down the wooden steps of the pavilion. Daniel knew someday soon Marg would ask for permission to attend the weekend dances at the gardens. But for now, she was still one of his little girls. All three were dressed up for this special day. Flo and Dorothy still wore large satin bows in their hair. Marg's hair was piled softly on top of her head, reminding Dan-iel of Hattie in their younger years.

Even though there were people all around, there was still a

stove available, and no one was near it yet. Hattie spread the blanket and Daniel put on the pasties to heat. Old friends from church arrived and shared the stove and picnic table.

Each girl had money for two rides. The roller coaster was Marg's favorite. She loved the tingle in her stomach after the slow climb to the first peak, then that incredible drop down and the screech of the cars as they whizzed round a corner. This was the reason for the pulled back and pinned hairdo—it would stay in place for the windy ride.

Flo liked the airplane rides and Dorothy loved the carousel. The horses were suited for all personalities. Dorothy loved the small horse with the gently tilted head. The rein hung loosely from its soft mouth. Marg's bright yellow carousel horse contrasted greatly with the dark, wild-eyed steed in the next row.

The happy mood at the gardens did not hint at the turmoil that was going on in the world. Daniel couldn't help but remember the past week. There was unrest everywhere. The United States officially went to war with

FAMILY PHOTO AT COLUMBIA GARDENS (MOST UNIDENTIFIED). LOWER RIGHT: HATTIE IN FRONT HOLDING DOROTHY CLANCY. DANIEL JOHN CLANCY IN THE BACK ROW.

DESTINATION: BUTTE, MONTANA

Germany on April 6, 1917. Though the mines were working at an intense pace, the war divided normally patriotic Butte, notably causing some grumbling among the Irish-Americans, who did not like siding with the British under any circumstances.

Daniel pulled out the newspaper and began to read the war news. As a silent protest against the British, not many bonds had been sold in Butte, but Hattie and her brothers, sister, and mother felt tied to Wales.

Hattie had cried over the many lives destroyed by the war. Now, one of her own was heading out. After the day at the gardens, the Clancys joined all of the Davis families gathered at Margaret's home to see Syl off and wish him a safe return. Syl and Rose and their three daughters, Rosemary, Joan, and Sylvia were the guests of honor. Margaret Davis was now married to a much younger man, John Williams. Daniel pretended to talk to Tommy about math because he didn't want to talk about the war. The mood in the

DAVIS FAMILY GATHERING BEFORE SYL DAVIS LEAVES FOR WORLD WAR I. FRONT ROW FROM LEFT: CLARA AND WILL DAVIS, FLORENCE DAVIS, MARGARET DAVIS (NOW MARGARET WILLIAMS), DOROTHY AND HATTIE CLANCY. BACK ROW: THOMAS DAVIS, ROSE AND SYL DAVIS, DANIEL CLANCY, AND JOHN WILLIAMS.

mine had been somber, and Daniel wanted to avoid that discussion as well.

After the gathering, Hattie and Daniel returned home with the girls. At 11:45 p.m., the whistle at the Speculator Mine began to blow. It began like a wail. Every woman who lived near the mines grabbed a shawl and ran out in the night. Children were left in their beds if older siblings were there. Hattie ran toward the sound, joined by many of her neighbors. Silence was everywhere. Suddenly, the sight of smoke from the Speculator and the Granite Mountain Mine and the blare of more whistles broke the stillness. Surrounded by the shrill sounds and the dark night, the Irish women began to keen; some people stood frozen.

Hattie whispered to herself, "Thank God Daniel's not on shift at the Speculator tonight," as she headed for the fences surrounding the mine. With demand for copper high because of the war, the mines were running around the clock, seven days a week. More than 400 men were working underground when the fire started. Above ground the women began praying and rushed home to bring back the food they knew would be needed for the rescue efforts.

Inside the mine, an inferno raged. The assistant foreman, Ernest Sallau, had descended the Granite Mountain shaft to recheck a damaged electrified cable. At about 2,500 feet below the surface, his carbide lamp accidentally touched the cable's oil-soaked insulation and sparked a fire. Fed by the updraft, flames climbed the cable and reached to the surface. The mine timbers, soaked in creosote and other chemicals, burst into flames. Soon, flames, smoke, and noxious gasses spread through horizontal crosscuts to the Speculator shaft.

Some miners were able to escape through the High Ore Mine, but many miners remained trapped below. Some sought refuge behind sealed doors and bulkheads at different levels in the mine. Others built makeshift barriers against the smoke and gas out of timbers, canvas, and any other materials they could scavenge. At midnight, twenty-four hours after the fire's onset, they were clamoring to break the barrier and take a chance to find freedom from the stifling atmosphere of the refuge chamber where the men slowly were sapping oxygen from the air. Manus Duggan realized that this was the only place where there was any possibility of surviving. He racked his brain to think of any way to conserve the limited air.[1]

"An hour after the fire started, 29 men, under the leadership of Manus Duggan, entered a crosscut. . . and built a bulkhead of timber, canvas, clothing, and dirt which kept out the gas and protected them for a day and a half until the air in the level had been cleared of the poisonous fumes so that they were enabled to reach the shaft and be taken to a place of safety."[2]

Manus Duggan was "the first to mount the barrier they had made and with three others started for the entrance to the crosscut. That was the last seen of him by his former companions. The remaining 25 men later reached the shaft and were hoisted to the surface, where they were saved."[3]

As men worked to save the miners, James D. Moore, shift boss, wrote letters to his wife in his time book:

"In the dark we are dying—Your loving Jim.

"Dear Pet, this may be the last message you get from me. The gas broke about 11:15 p.m. I tried to get all the men out, but the smoke was too strong. I got some of the boys with me in a drift and put in a bulkhead . . . if anything happens to me you had better sell the house . . . and go to California. You will know your Jim died like a man and his last thought was for his wife that I love better than anyone on earth . . . . We will meet again. Tell mother and the boys goodbyes. Wish love to my pet and may God take care of you."[4]

For two days, rescue crews searched for survivors, bringing up body after body. The death toll climbed. But on June 10, 1917, twenty-five of the men with Manus Duggan were rescued from the Speculator Mine. Duggan had led the men to a safe exit, but he was trapped by the fumes and died. "The last man to see Manus Duggan was John McGarvey and he said that the hero of the catastrophe was staggering at that time as though he had become weakened.

"Murty Shea, one of the rescued men, joined the others in praise of Manus Duggan. Mr. Shea saw Duggan making out his will to his wife, and a message to her. Duggan tried to hide his writing hoping to keep up the courage of the others."[5]

The letters to his wife found in his pocket began:

"To my Dear Wife and Mother: It takes my heart away to be taken from you so suddenly and unexpectedly, but think not of me for if death comes, it will be in a sleep without suffering.

"I ask forgiveness for any suffering or pain I have ever caused. Madge, dear, the place [the Duggan home at 1010 Zarelda] is for you and the child. Manus"[6]

Some of the bodies showed the incredible struggle the men had endured before they died. Fingers were torn to the bone from attempts to claw the concrete bulkheads. The Copper Kings had not foreseen that their efforts to keep out thieves would lead to this incredible tragedy.

The newspaper offices posted hourly bulletins: "A Public Morgue Established at Mine: Bodies Taken from Hysterical Families Mobbed the Morgues and Undertaking Places. Women and Children Showed the Terror of Life Without Support."[7]

Mayor Maloney received a message from Missoula Mayor H. T. Wilkinson that the people of Missoula were dispatching a ton of flowers for those lost in the Speculator fire. The flowers were being sent by the Missoula Chamber of Commerce and were brought in from the gardens and yards of Missoula residents. A. Cobban, a former Butte resident who remembered the dearth of flowers in Butte at the time of the 1895 mine explosion, inspired the campaign.[8] Thousands of Butte residents paid their respects to Manus Duggan for his heroism. In all, 168 men died in the Speculator fire.

BRAVE MEN RESPOND TO SIGNAL OF THOSE IMPRISONED IN MINE

Hope Revives After Hours of Effort When Bell From the 2,400 Level Tells of Presence of Those Almost Given Up for Lost. Two Go Down in "Chippy" Skip and Bring Men to Surface. Imprisoned Victims Are Overjoyed to Meet Their Rescuers.

SPECULATOR MINE DISASTER

SCENE DURING RESCUE WORK AT THE NORTH BUTTE

RESCUE WORK AT THE SPECULATOR MINE

CHAPTER 18 ᔡ

UNION CONFLICT

ᔡ

There was distrust and unrest among the miners following the Speculator disaster. After the fire had been extinguished, Daniel and the rest of the miners worried until the union implemented new safety measures; however, the unions were still turbulent.

The Metal Mine Workers called a strike, demanding wages of $6 per day irrespective of the price of copper. Martial law was again invoked.

In August, Daniel Clancy opened the newspaper to read about the hanging of union organizer, Frank Little. Miners were speculating about what really happened.

"Armed Vigilantes Lynch I.W.W. Leader," read the headline in *The Butte Miner.*

"Frank H. Little, a member of the executive board and a recognized leader of the I.W.W., who recently was deported from Arizona because of his activities in the district, was lynched at about 3:00 o'clock yesterday morning by six or seven armed, masked, unknown men, so-called vigilantes who took him by surprise in his room."[1]

The act horrified many, including U.S. District Attorney

B. K. Wheeler, who issued a statement: "I consider the act of the band of men who murdered Little a most seditious and devilish piece of business and one that all decent citizens will brand as a stain and disgrace on the city."[2]

The newspaper article documented the terror of Frank Little. "The Vigilantes took Little by surprise, and attired in only his undergarments, he was placed in a waiting automobile and rushed to the site chosen for his execution. There, after a desperate struggle, the fatal noose was placed around his neck and he was dropped from the fourteen-foot trestle to his death. Little died instantly for his neck was broken."[3]

The turmoil and terror of 1917 shook Butte to the core. Daniel Clancy thought he would be happy to see the year end. He suspected the rest of Butte felt the same way.

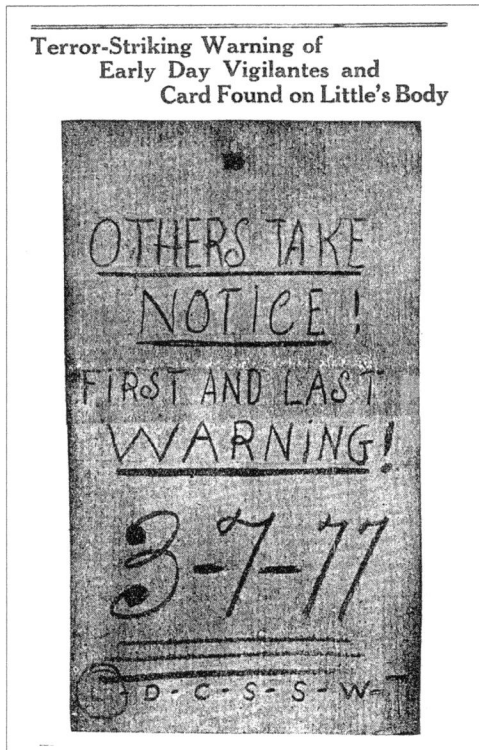

Terror-Striking Warning of
Early Day Vigilantes and
Card Found on Little's Body

OTHERS TAKE NOTICE!
FIRST AND LAST WARNING!
3-7-77
D-C-S-S-W

FOUND ON FRANK LITTLE'S BODY
HANGED ON A TRAIN TRESTLE

CHAPTER 19 ᕲ

DANNY IS BORN

———————————————————————————— ᕲ

T oil and turmoil were not the only things growing in Butte. Hattie was pregnant with her fourth child, and everything seemed to be going along fairly well as she tended her household and continued to do her sewing.

Although she hadn't really cared about the gender of her first three babies, she now thought it would be nice to have a son. She asked Daniel what they should name the baby. Hattie said she would like to name a son, William, for her father. Daniel glanced at her, but did not respond. He had been named for his father, John Daniel, and thought his son should also bear the names of his father and grandfather.

Hattie said if the baby were a girl, she'd like to name her Caitlin because it combined their Welsh and Irish ancestry, but Daniel disagreed, saying people would not be able to tell which nationality she was. Besides, he did not think the two names were a good match—Caitlin Clancy. The subject was dropped, and Hattie focused on her three daughters.

Grandmother Margaret loved babies as much as Hattie, but she was concerned about this pregnancy. Hattie already was so busy she didn't even have time to read or put up her feet. Margaret told Marg, Flo, and Dorothy to help their mother as much as possible. They loved sitting with her. She seemed bigger with this baby, and her energy wasn't where it should have been. It took longer to complete washing and sewing, and even to tell the old stories.

Daniel seemed remote. The mines, now owned by Amalgamated, tended to elicit fear instead of loyalty. When she first told Daniel about the baby, he looked startled. She knew there had been few intimate moments, but he seemed almost puzzled about how this could have happened.

When Hattie again brought up the subject of names, he said it didn't matter. She hoped this child would favor Daniel's ancestry more. True, they were both Celts, but there were noticeable differences. Daniel had never been the robust, outgoing Irishman he might have been if he had not lived in the orphanage. The heart seemed to be out of him.

In October, a son was born. "Ah, Daniel, he looks so like you," Hattie gasped when she first saw the baby. Daniel couldn't speak. He did love the three little girls, but wanted to have the Clancy name continue. Daniel asked if Hattie wanted to name the baby for her father. Hattie said she would rather name their son Daniel John Clancy. They would call him Danny.

For the first time in a long time, Daniel smiled. Hattie had forgotten how handsome Daniel could look when he was relaxed.

FROM LEFT: MARG, HATTIE HOLDING DANNY, FLO, AND DOROTHY

CHAPTER 20 ೩೨

INFLUENZA AND THE SLOWDOWN OF MINING

The beginning of 1918 proved to be less dramatic than 1917, but it was still intense. On January 14, 1918, John O'Neill, Frank Fisher, and Sherman Powell, a black man, were hanged in the yard of the courthouse. It was Butte's first and only triple hanging. By February, there were many meatless meals, a sacrifice made so Butte could lead the nation in the purchase of Liberty bonds. In November, the Armistice was signed, and Butte celebrated for three days and nights.

In December 1918, an influenza epidemic hit Butte hard, with five out of seven families falling ill. There were three or four funerals per day. Hattie and her family were under quarantine because one of Daniel's partners in the mine had died from the influenza.

An old schoolhouse was turned over to the Red Cross to serve as an auxiliary hospital, since the others in the city were full. The back door was where the undertaker came to pick up the dead.

Dr. Riley worked hour after hour. The lamps were covered

with tissue paper to shield the sick and the dying from the glare.[1] There were impromptu weddings, and some reconciliations were forged between estranged families. Thomas Flynn had fought with his brother, Seamus, for years over who should have stayed in Ireland with their mother, Mary. Seamus was in the final throes of the influenza when Thomas came to his bedside.

More than 300 Butte residents died from the epidemic. Everybody wore camphor necklaces. The grocery boy had a big mask over his mouth and nose made from a bag of camphor tied around his neck. Two of Hattie's friends, a husband and wife, passed away just days apart. The wife's name was Sara, Hattie's friend from their working days at Paumie Dye House. She had two boys, Phil and John, a daughter, Angela, and a new baby, Beth. The two daughters also succumbed to the influenza and were buried with Sara, the baby in her arms. Hattie cried when she read about Sara's death.

Daniel and Hattie passed the time quarantined with the children by playing games and taking turns reading stories.

CHAPTER 21 ᘛ

THE TONG WARS

I
n 1921, the Chinese Tong Wars affected all of Butte. Daniel avidly read *The Butte Miner* and *The Anaconda Standard* to find out what was happening. The first trouble began on October 14, 1921, when Chong Song, first president of Bing Kong Tong, was mysteriously shot at 10 p.m.

"The assassins apparently laid in wait in the shadows of the east side of China [A]lley across from Song's house. One bullet, which either passed through the victim's body or went wild struck the glass in the door of the Wah Chong Tai company under Mai Wah noodle parlor and continued on, to be embedded in a long board hanging from the ceiling. It was found to be of .38 caliber.

"The shots were heard for a number of blocks, and were estimated from eight to ten.

"Chinatown was being scoured by police and members of the sheriff's office within a few minutes of the shooting. Residents of the district were in a state of fear, which clung during the past several weeks after the shooting.

"In the 100 block of China [A]lley, a door was dashed down

by Chief Murphy and others, and Quang Long Chang, who was in the place, was arrested. He is said to be one of the leaders of a tong that is a rival to the one to which the dead man belonged.

"Friday evening Butte's Chinatown, for eight months in a state of three tong killings in that time, showed activity for the first time."[1]

With little information except that found in the newspapers, most of Butte only guessed at the terror of the Tong Wars. As time passed, Daniel continued to follow the story.

On February 13, "1922, Hum Mon Sin, ro Hum Tong, 60 years, a merchant here for 40 years, was shot down by a pair of gunmen, who fired a fusillade into their victim's back as he sauntered from his house, 207 China [A]lley, puffing a long oriental pipe. A 'cowboy Chinaman' and a stocky accomplice are being hunted by the officers a result of the affair, which marked the fourth mysterious Chinese murder in little more than a year.

"The dead man was a close friend of Chong Song, who was shot down by gunmen in front of his house on South Wyoming Street, Oct. 14, and had been acting as an administrator of the Chong estate.

"But one witness of the killing has been found. A short, nervous Chinaman told officers that he was on the corner of the alley and on his way to the business place of the slain man when the shots rang out and he saw two men firing at their victim. That he can identify the gunmen is the statement of the Chinese to officers and upon this man largely lie the authorities' hopes of solving the murder."[2]

The Friday morning article, February 17, 1922, from *The Butte Miner* entitled "All Butte Now in Chinese Tong War," expressed the reality that the entire town was feeling the impact of the conflict. "Due to the Tong War, and the fear of delivering goods, citizens were told not to expect perfect laundry in less than a week."[3]

The Tong War ended June 24, 1922, when a pact between the factions was signed in San Francisco. After eight months, Butte's Chinatown returned to normal.[4]

SCENE OF BUTTE'S LATEST CHINESE OUTBREAK

CHINA ALLEY, WHERE MON SING WAS SHOT DOWN.
Crosses show: No. 1—Mon Sing's shop. No. 2—Where Mon Sing was passing when assassins opened fire. No. 3—Telegraph pole beside which murderers stood.

CHAPTER 22

1924

Marg, Flo, Dorothy, and Danny were all excited when Hattie told them the family would have another new baby. The pregnancy went along quite well, but Hattie frequently seemed tired.

She scheduled a midwife because her sister Florence was too busy with her own two sons. Hattie's mother, Margaret, was so negative about another baby that Hattie decided to not ask her for help.

Mary O'Brien was to help with the delivery and the care of the family. Hattie asked Daniel about names for the baby. Daniel thought they should name the baby Adeline—Hattie's full name—if they had a girl. If the baby were a boy, they would name him William, after Hattie's father and brother. When little Adeline was born, Hattie loved holding her and being surrounded by Marg, Flo, Dorothy, and Danny.

Not long after, Hattie and Daniel walked around their yard. The melting snow and faint shoots of grass were the result of a false spring. Hattie couldn't wait to plant her marigolds. As she walked, her legs ached. Her right leg seemed to have a swollen spot. The doctor told Hattie to rest and be patient because there was a blood clot in her leg.

Daniel was antsy. He couldn't stand to be around sick people, and Hattie had never been sick. He didn't know why he felt anxious, but he was eager to have the family back to normal again.

Hattie hugged each child every time they passed by. She caressed the baby's cheeks, and even some of the Welsh poetry came back to her as she spoke softly to Adeline.

One day, Hattie told the children that Papa would take the girls to town the next day to get Easter shoes. Daniel made Hattie an eggnog at 4 a.m. She called him at 7 a.m. and said she didn't feel well and couldn't breathe. Daniel went next door to call the doctor. Hattie died at nine o'clock in the morning.

Will and Syl were called. Tommy took the streetcar to pick up Auntie Florence. Sadly, one loss was followed by another. While Florence was on her way to help Hattie's family, she and her family lost their home to a fire.

Hattie was buried in Mount Moriah cemetery, which had grown quite large due to the influenza epidemic and all of the mine disasters. Hattie's marker was made of granite. Daniel picked out an unusual shape, and four abstract flowers were the only adornment on the stone that was inscribed with Hattie's name and the years she lived. Her funeral was on an early spring day, a dismal, blustery day in Butte. The Catholic cemetery was next to Mount Moriah, separated only by a wrought iron fence. There could be no blessing for Hattie by a priest because she had never converted to Catholicism.

CHAPTER 23 ꩜

SURVIVAL FOR THE CLANCY FAMILY

Hattie's brother Will and her sister-in-law Clara took in Adeline and Danny right after the funeral. Their boys were raised, and they were delighted to have children in their home again. Clara especially loved taking care of Adeline. As she dried the baby's toes one by one, Clara told Will that she never knew how much she would enjoy holding and cuddling a baby again. Will thought Adeline was a darling baby—so bright-eyed. Danny seemed comfortable, but every few days he needed to return home to see his father and older sisters. Clara hoped they would be able to adopt the children.

For six months, the arrangement worked, but one day in September, Daniel went to visit his children. Adeline was on her blanket on the floor. She held her head high and looked ready to take off in a fast crawl. Clara asked her where Daddy was. Adeline's eyes glanced past Daniel Clancy and fixed on Will Davis. Adeline cooed and smiled happily. Daniel jumped up and said, "That's it! I am her father. I'm taking my children home with me. Get your clothes, Danny."[1]

A few weeks later, a meeting was called between Daniel and Auntie Florence. It was decided that Florence, her husband, Charlie, and their two sons, Elroy and Leonard, would move into the Clancy home. Florence and Charlie would take care of the household because Daniel was being sent to Galen by the Anaconda Company for consumption due to silicosis from the mines. Galen had been built in 1911 to care for patients with tuberculosis, but now miners were sent there to recuperate.

When Daniel arrived at Galen, he willed his lungs to expand more and more, but his lungs would not cooperate. Daniel was assigned to the men's quarters in Byron Hall. There were separate quarters for men, women, and children. Men primarily were the ones suffering from silicosis, but tuberculosis struck females, males, and even children.

Daniel took in the grounds in a quick glance. "It's like I'm a ten-year-old again in another location miles from town," he thought.

Galen was fifty miles from Butte and twelve miles south of Deer Lodge, the site of the Montana State Prison. As far as Daniel was concerned, Galen was a prison. He wanted to be home with his children.

Three times a day, he had to sit in front of the machine that was working to heal his lungs. The machine was approximately four feet high. It was a cylinder and had a two-foot tube that secreted medicine into his lungs to make breathing easier.

After three weeks, he received a letter from home. Marg, Flo, and Dorothy all wrote notes. Danny did not. Daniel felt very far away and longed to hold Adeline in his arms.

The area surrounding Galen was flatter than Butte. There was fresh air, almost too fresh in Daniel's estimation. The air smelled like the agricultural center that it was. It reminded Daniel of his brief, early years at St. Joseph's Orphanage with its animals and farm-like setting.

One day, while feeling sorry for himself, he noticed the sad children in the tuberculosis wing. Daniel could visit with them through the glass. He came to enjoy cheering up the little ones, but still ached for his own children in Butte.

When he completed the series of treatments, Daniel felt stronger than he had in years. He was sent home. He prayed that he would be able to return to work in the mine full time. He knew it was difficult for everyone, with Charlie and Auntie Florence trying to care for their own sons and five Clancy children.

Daniel returned to work, but after two months, the terrible convulsive coughing began again. He tried to cover up his coughs, but at night when the house was still, it was impossible for anyone to sleep. He was sleeping on a cot in the living room. Florence, Charlie, and baby Adeline used his and Hattie's old bedroom. Danny and his two cousins were sharing a room, and the three older girls shared another. Marg, Flo, Dorothy, Danny, and their cousins Elroy and Leonard were all in school.

After fifteen months, Charlie was offered a postmaster's position in Anaconda. Florence offered to take the Clancys with them, but Daniel wanted to hold out and keep his family together. He planned to take them to St. Joseph's Orphanage in Helena, so the children could all be together until he was well.

Before school started, Miss Jackson, a teacher, visited the Clancys and told Marg she could go to school half days. Unfortunately, there was no one to take care of Adeline. It ended up that Dorothy and Daniel attended school, while Marg and Flo took care of Adeline.

That first Christmas without Hattie, Marg answered the door as the rest of the family decorated the Christmas tree. The Josher's Club, a group of generous citizens, which began on Christmas Day in 1892, brought in big boxes of groceries.

Marg tried to keep the family together as she had promised her mother, but it was too much for her. Daniel had her call Mrs. Phillips, who worked in the courthouse and was in the Human Services Department. She helped place Adeline and Danny in the Paul Clark Home.

Daniel told all of his children to be strong, because they would be back together as soon as he was well. He quietly repeated the prayer: "God fits the back to the burden."[2]

For the time being, Marg would rent an apartment and work at Gamer's Bakery. Florence would live with her grandmother, Margaret Davis Williams, and Uncle Tommy Davis. Dorothy would move in with and work for a Butte family, and Danny and Adeline would live at the Paul Clark Home, which was not considered an orphanage because children had to have one living parent to be admitted.

The Clancy furniture was taken to the courthouse for storage. All of the packing was completed while Daniel was back in Galen for more treatments. Auntie Florence was sad as she took Danny and Adeline up the steps to the Paul Clark Home.

"What is the name of this street?" asked Danny, who had not been this far on the west side of town.

"It's Excelsior Street," said Auntie Florence.

"What a long name for a street," said Danny as he and Adeline climbed the steep stairs to the massive three-story building that was now their new home.

DANNY CLANCY, THE ONLY BOY WITH THE GIRLS, AT THE MAY DAY CELEBRATION AT COLUMBIA GARDENS

LIFE AT THE PAUL CLARK HOME

T he brick building had been occupied since William A. Clark donated it to the Associated Charities many years ago. Danny was immediately drawn to the library with classical books by Victor Hugo and William Shakespeare's sonnets.

Daniel paid $10 per month for the care of his two youngest children, Adeline and Danny. There was a large black ledger where payments were posted monthly. Efficiency and education were the order at the Paul Clark Home. There were classes conducted in the basement for young men to learn trades, and young women learned homemaking skills. Since the Clancy family was Catholic, the tuition for the Catholic schools would be free.

Social activities included open houses to honor Paul Clark, the son of William A. Clark, who had died so young. Danny was not entirely comfortable with those events since it pointed out the many children who were not orphans, but needed to live in the home because their families could not care for them.

Adeline and Danny were confidants, with only the dormitory lockers serving to divide the boy's and the girl's quarters. Rows of sinks in the bathrooms and the rows of iron beds accommodated children in the home. Years passed with children quarantined whenever measles, mumps, or chickenpox appeared on a child. Danny never caught these childhood illnesses, so he kept up well with his classes.

DANNY AND ADELINE CLANCY OUTSIDE THE PAUL CLARK HOME

CHAPTER 25 ♪

THE YOUNG ADULT YEARS

———————————————————————————————— ♪

Years passed by as years do. As a Paul Clark Home resident who was Catholic, Danny attended Boys Central High School tuition free. Daily he and Adeline saw each other at the home while she attended Franklin School. Dorothy was living with Margaret, her grandmother, and Uncle Tommy in the Davis family home; Flo was dating a young man, Lewis Schneller; and Marg was still working at Gamer's Bakery and living in the Leonard Apartments. Life certainly had changed for the Clancy family, with everyone living apart except for Adeline and Danny, who remained at the Paul Clark Home until graduation from high school. Their father, Daniel, was working at Galen with the children and those in the respiratory wings. Auntie Florence was living in Anaconda with Charlie and her sons, Elroy and Leonard, the latter weak from the effects of scarlet fever.

Danny's best friends from Butte Central, Albert Ciabattari and Bob Osier, would be great friends for all of his life. Bob did not have siblings, so Danny was always welcome to stay at the Everett home at Columbia Gardens. Bob's father had died, so his mother, Mary, married Bill Everett, who tended the flowers at the gardens. Their red wooden home had a chicken coop in the back where Danny and Bob collected eggs for breakfast. Danny was always hungry for cereal and milk, especially before bed.

He did not remember all of the joyous times his family and grandparents had spent at the gardens, but he was making his own memories. Later in high school, Albert (nicknamed Bat), Danny, and Bob were among those who danced away the nights at the Columbia Gardens Dance Pavilion. Danny and James Bertoglio sang in the Glee Club one year, and as seniors their graduation photographs and lists of accomplishments were noted in the *Maroon,* the Butte Central yearbook. A motto was included under each boy's photo. James's motto was "He is the lord of his soul." Danny's motto, "I was not always a man of woe," hinted at the early events in his life. The seniors of 1935 appeared in the "Class Prophecy" written by John H. Mack and Albert Weaver. "Our beloved president, Jimmie Bertoglio, as the owner of the Grappo Products, Inc. Prosperous and happy as ever, Jim is the wine baron of Meaderville. . . . Bobby Osier and Dan Clancy are aldermen in Anaconda. They spent so much time in that fair city that the city adopted them."[1]

Daniel exacted a promise from Danny that he would never work in the mines, so Danny set his sights on attending college to become an accountant. The trustees of the Paul Clark Home encouraged students who would benefit from schooling past high school. Although Danny's goal was college, the trustees thought Butte Business College would be ideal. Danny studied accounting and excelled at the college.

He and four friends found an apartment. Danny's job was at the Red Rooster, where he worked with Joe Casne, another Italian friend. They loved the friendliness of the place. Danny also worked at the American Theater, where he could enjoy movies every night of the week. He imagined himself as the debonair hero in many romantic movies.

The movies turned into reality when the United States went to war. In October 1941, Congress passed the Conscription Act whereby young men would be given a number and there would be a drawing. Those whose numbers were drawn had to give one year of military service. Two months later,

DANIEL J. CLANCY
"Dan"
Hobby: Fox trots.
"I was not always a man of woe."
Maroon, '34, '35.
Glee Club, '34.

CHARLES R. CHOQUETTE
"Chuck"
Hobby: Acting.
"The world's a stage on which all parts are played."
Honor Student, '32, '33, '34, '35.
Dramatic Club, '32, '33, '34, '35.
Dancing, '32, '33.
Maroon Staff, '34, '35.
Glee Club, '35.

WILLARD M. BOAM
"Bud"
Hobby: Taking care of Freel.
"All truths are not to be told."
Honor Student, '32, '35.
Football, '33, '34.
Scepters, '32, '33, '34, '35.
Gymnastics, '34, '35.
Monogram Club, '34, '35.

JAMES S. BERTOGLIO
"Bert"
Hobby: Field and stream.
"He is the lord of his soul."
Honor Student, '32, '33, '34, '35.
Class Officer, '35.
Monogram Club, '35.
Gymnastics, '35.
Football, '34.
Glee Club, '34.

1935

Page Ten

THE MAROON PHOTOS

Pearl Harbor was attacked. Danny was being sent to Fort Lewis, Washington. His four sisters, his father, and his aunts and uncles were at the Butte railroad station to see him off. Danny told Adeline "he prayed God would let him live so he could come home, find a nice Catholic girl, get married, and have children and have a home of his own."[2] Adeline did not see Danny for four years.

V·MAIL

DANIEL CLANCY SR. AND DANNY CLANCY JR. BEFORE WWII

PART VI

CHAPTER 26

DANNY AND WORLD WAR II 1942

Danny Clancy would not return to Butte, Montana, for four years but Butte was never far from his mind, as reflected in the letters to his sister, Dorothy, who kept the letters that follow for more than forty years.

July 5, 1942

Dear Pop:

I tried to write to you before this but just haven't had time. The morning before last we got two hours notice that we were pulling out so I didn't have time to write. couldn't even stop at the telegraph office in Manchester to pick up the telegram. I've asked Postal to transfer it down here but so far it hasn't arrived. The base here seems to be nice but it is spread over the state of Connecticut. On top of that, it is so well camouflaged it's hard to find the barracks.

I'm not going to make this very long cause we've been working ever since we got here and I haven't even had a chance to get my—[1]

Friday, Aug. 20, 1942

Dear Dot:

Had a nice surprise yesterday when I received a letter from Johnny O'Neal. Gee that's the first I've had in over a year. He is the civilian manager of the PX at Fort Harrison in Helena. Says he is working like the devil but the money is good and of course, he isn't in the army. I guess I told you that they had another baby, didn't I? He asked me if there was anything he could get out of the PX there so I'll probably be able to get a camera now.

I met that kid from Butte, Johnny Fallon, again last week. We had a very good time drinking a toast to the natives of Butte. However, we didn't get drunk. Gee, it's good to talk to someone from Butte.

Holy smoke, Dot, things are sure getting tough on the folks back home. Only one pint of whiskey per week per person. Old soaks like us couldn't get by on that, could we?

I don't know whether I told you or not that I received some pictures of Harry Jay that Marg sent. He is sure a cute tyke and fat as any-thing. Wonder what Marg is feeding him.

Adeline doesn't seem to like Los Angeles, does she. Guess she's just a hill-billy like the rest of us.

I've got so damn many letters to answer it isn't funny and I never seem to get at any of them. I get lazier as time goes on. When I think of about two more years overseas I just about pull my hair out. I sure do wish those guys would give up, don't you?

Well, Dot, I'll close this now and try to write more next time.

Bye-now

Love

Dan²

Friday, Aug. 29, 1942

Dear Dot:

Sorry I haven't written for so long but guess you understand how it was. I received your last letter two days before I left. It was impossible to call home. Things like that just aren't being done.

Haven't heard from Marg for a long time. The last letter I had was dated July 28. I sure hope that she's okay.

I've been on K.P. this week so there's not much I can tell you of interest. I sure hate potatoes. We're eating American rations now and the food is really as good as we had in the U.S.

Last Saturday I went to town. Didn't see much cause I didn't get there until after ten o'clock. The city is about five miles from here and we walked all the way. Saw several nice looking girls.

Glad to hear that Smitty is doing so well. Looks like our men will be buck privates for the duration. But who cares. Someone has to be. Can't have an army of generals.

Did Doris quit the theater? I had a post card from her when I went to Conn. She said that she'd write a letter later. If you see her or write to her, give her my address.

In my letter to Pa I told him to send me a carton of cigs every week and also a box of candy bars. Don't send them quite so often, but whenever you have them insured.

Well, Dot, I've got to close. There's just nothing to write about except the weather and that's not so hot. Best I stop this and get some tea.

There's no need for worry, Dot, don't.

Love,

Dan [3]

_____

Oct. 29, 1942

Dear Dot:

Guess what day this is? Yep, you're correct. It is my birthday- and don't even have a cake. I celebrated two nights ago. I had my dates all mixed. Another kid and myself had dinner with some friends, and then we all went to a pub. Yesterday morning I woke up with a head like a baboon.

Haven't heard from Marg since the baby was born. Hope everything is okay. Suppose so or I'd have had word. Anyway, I probably won't even know his name for a long time now.

In case you go through with your plans to get married, good luck. I think it's a swell idea. Hope Smitty won't have to leave the country. It'll be swell if he can stay where he is.

So now Val is a mama. With her temper she'll probably throw it out the window some night when it starts to cry.

Bert Henson should do a nice business now with no competition.

Wish I knew if Flo received the money I cabled home. Also, if she's receiving my allotment. If you need any money, help yourself to whatever there is. More than likely I won't receive any mail that was sent to A.P.P. 1255 or 637. Be sure to use 525 for my APO Number. Wonder what the idea of changing it is.

Well Dot, I'm exhausted for news. I'll write again as soon as possible. Regards to Smitty.

Love

Dan[4]

Somewhere in U. W. Africa

Dec. 9, 1942

Dear Dotty:

Just finished writing to Flo & Marg, and so now must write to you. This having my family scattered all over the country isn't so hot when I have to start writing letters. But it'll be swell when I come home and can spend two or three months a year visiting each of you. So, I guess writing these few extra letters is worth it. I'm taking for granted that you're now married and living in Sunny California. Here's hoping that it doesn't rain there as much as it did last year in the sunny South. Oh, well, Dot, whatever you're doing, I hope you're happy. I spent the whole day reading a book titled: "Marriage is a Private Affair." It was damn good and I had a very enjoyable time. In fact, if I had a good book to read every day, the time would go much faster and I wouldn't be wishing for you so much. Unfortunately though, reading material is very limited. Last week I went to town and bought a Christmas present but you'll have to wait till I come home to get it. I have so many things I want to take home that I'll have to throw away most of my clothes to make room. Holy smoke, maybe I ought to wait until the war is over before I think of going home but that's all we ever talk of. Yep, Dot, the States is a wonderful place and anybody living there is pretty lucky. Guess it's well worth fighting for too. The last letter I had from you was the one in which you told me about Marg having a baby that day. Haven't had any mail dated later than that. So, no doubt I have quite a lot of it between England, the States, and here someplace. Hope it catches up with me soon. Hope Smitty is _ by now. Hello to him.

Be good. I'll write again next week.

Love

Dan[5]

CHAPTER 27 ꙮ

DANNY AND WORLD WAR II 1943

V-Mail

Jan. 5, 1943

Dear Dot & Smitty: Just received your letter today saying that you are now in Texas. What a state to live in. Thanks very much for your Christmas present. It reached me a few days after Christmas. The cig lighter was just what I was praying for. So far, I've received 11 packages. If that isn't doing good, I'll quit. Everyone in my tent 'cept me is from Texas. Think we don't go round and round? Bye for now—Love, D[6]

U. W. Africa

Friday, Jan. 8, 1943

Dear Dot:

Thought that the next letter I wrote to you would be addressed to Mrs. Smith but I see by your letter that it's still Miss Clancy. What are you doing? Playing hard to get?

You said that Smitty had a furlough. It's hard to believe. I haven't even had a twenty-four hour pass since I've been in the army. Course, he's a salesman. Bet you did have fun visiting with Marg & Harry. Glad she's feeling so good. She seems to be very well pleased with herself now that she has her baby. Hope she doesn't go through with her plans to have three more. Holy smoke, I'll be forty years old by the time I come home if I keep worrying about her and her babies.

All of my Christmas packages are a little late in arriving. Nine I know have been sent. I'm beginning to think they're at the bottom of the ocean.

Next time you write, send a few air mails stamps. I'm borrowing off of everybody in camp. Also, send a couple good snapshots of yourself. I've been bragging on what good-looking sisters I have, but I've no proof.

Guess this is all Dorothy. Regards to Smitty. Love to you

Dan[7]

PHOTO FROM AFRICA, A FELLOW SOLDIER, JIM FROM IDAHO, CLIMBED THE TREE

Tuesday, Jan. 20, 1943

Dear Sis & Brother-in-law:

Boy, oh boy, Smitty, you don't know what you've gotten yourself in for. Maybe you didn't know it, but after this short career of mine in the army, I plan to spend the rest of my natural life living off my family. Course I'm not very expensive. In all seriousness, though, I'm very glad for both of you. I hope you'll be very happy. This member of the family approves. There's only four others. I'd like to send a present but right now it's impossible.

Nothing new from this part of the world. Everything is quite dull.

Some of my Christmas packages have arrived. That is four of them. One from Marg, Tom & Ernesta, Dan & Erma Sullivan, and also a box of Gamer's candy with no name in it. Wish the rest would get here. Dot, why don't you prove you're a good cook now and send me some cookies.

Do you ever hear from any of the old gang? I never do. Jane used to write but I haven't heard from her for a long time. Did she get married?

Guess this is about all for now. Write as often as you can. I will as often as possible.

Love

Dan

P.S. Smitty, didn't I tell you that she snores something awful?[28]

Feb. 23, 1943

Dear Dot & Smitty—

Just finished writing to Pop and Marg so think I may as well go the rest of the way and assure you too that I'm in good health. I sure do wish that the family was together instead of all scattered out. It would be a lot simpler if I only had one letter to write each week instead of three or four. And, by the way, I haven't heard from you since that letter telling me you were married. I presume you're still married. Same old thing kids. No news. Outside of going to town last Thursday and seeing a show live on the fields on Friday everything is dull as H---. But we're in Africa so what can you expect. Sure hope this thing ends soon. I'm getting that feeling I'd like to go dancing and such.

Well, chums, think I'll close now and hope to hear from you soon.

Love, Dan [9]

Sunday, April 4, 1943

Dear Dot and Smitty:

Just received your letter dated Feb. 11. Seems like yours are getting through more regularly than Marg's now days. Hope you'll continue to write as often as you can.

Also, had a letter from Flo. Said I was going to be an uncle again soon. Gee, I sure wish people would stop having babies. They scare the devil out of me.

Was sure glad to hear that Pop is working again. Hope he'll hang on to this job. He'd better. Money is going to be hard to get after this war is over.

Boy, you're getting quite hefty aren't you? But you look a lot better for the extra weight. Think you'd better get a job though. It'll be pretty nice to have a few dollars put away when this is over to get a fresh start with.

No, I didn't receive any more packages. Guess they're all at the bottom of the ocean.

Went to town yesterday but didn't have such a good time. The gang I was with didn't want to do anything but drink and I'd rather take a dose of salts than drink the beer over here. Also, I always get sick when I drink wine so I was kind of bored. Got home about ten o'clock last night thoroughly tired, and I really slept. Guess that'll satisfy my desire to see civilian life for a month or so.

Well, kids, be good and write often.

Love

Dan

A.P.P. back to 525 again.[10]

Tuesday, June 7, 1943

Dear Dot & Smitty:

A week ago I wrote to you and said I'd write again in a few days. This doesn't seem like a few days but it is getting so hot here that I don't feel like doing anything. If it wasn't for keeping the family posted I don't think I'd write to anyone. It seems sort of silly. It's nice to keep in touch with everybody but I can't think of anything to write about. Usually every one of my letters are duplications.

A few months ago I sent a letter home with one of the pilots who was returning to the States, However, she evidently never received it for she has never mentioned it. Anyway it was supposed to be forwarded to you and Marg. I wrote of all the places I've been and what we've done. Sorry you didn't get it.

Someday when you have time try to find me a diary. Ever since I left the States I've been wishing I had one. I have kept notes though so I'll be able to write a summary of my life in the army. There are a few things I'll never forget. Especially the first bombing raid I went through. I'd never believe it was possible for a person to shake so much. But everyone else was the same way. The next day when we talked it over it was very funny but at the time we sure did a lot of praying. Early in the campaign we were stationed at one of the largest cities and it was being bombed every nite. Of course we were at a safe distance and as we just sat back and watched. One nite they bombed all the night and you should have seen the display. It would make all the fourth of July fireworks I've seen look like small fry. However, we've all had a lot of fun mixed in with a little misery. The misery consisted of the cold wet weather and the poor food. We had lamb stew twice a day seven days a week. I never did like lamb—now I hate it. I'm out of paper now so I guess I'll close now. Love—Dan [11]

Wednesday, Sept. 2, 1943

Dear Dot—

I seem to receive your mail a lot sooner than any of the others. Boy you can't imagine what an uneventful life I'm leading.

Last Sunday I went to Mass at a French farmhouse. An Italian priest who was a prisoner of war and couldn't speak a word of English heard my confession. A pilot who came out of the confessional ran up to another pilot and said, "Go ahead kid, you can tell everything. He can't speak a word of English." I sure had to laugh.

Well, Dot, I'll probably be seeing you about next August if I'm lucky. Don't look for this war with Germany to be over till next Fall. When they start sending % per month home, it'll take ten months for my name to come up. If I ever do get home they'll play like hell ever getting away from the States again. Think I'll go to bed now, Dot, must get up early.

Hello to Smitty.

Love, Dan[12]

Thursday, Sept. 9, 1943

Dear Dot—

Just getting out my weekly letters and of course you're on the list— so here goes. I'm sure I don't know why you even read them cause they're always the same. That's why it is so hard to write. There's never anything new or of interest to write about. Last night we had the picture "Casablanca." here at the field. It was sure good. We usually have a show twice a week—open air theatre—just drive right into it and sit in the truck. Before each show there is always a little "local talent" to keep us amused. Some of the men in the group have real talent. I wish I could do something. The news of Italy's surrender was well received here. It brings the end just a little closer. I'm now in hopes that we shall move into Italy. Boy, what I wouldn't give to see Rome and Vatican City. I think I'd die if we went to the Far East. I'd like to see India and China but I know if we did go there now we'd be stuck for the duration and that's too long. I still have hopes of coming home sometime next summer. Course, I had hopes of coming home this summer.

Well, Dot, bye for now. Write often

Love,[13]

Oct. 7, 1943

V-Mail

Dear Dot: Your letter dated Sept. reached me a few days ago. Your letters seem to be the only ones that are reaching me lately. I'd not use these forms but there isn't a lot of news. Ask Smitty if he can get "sweat shirts" in the PX. If so, how much. I want to get a couple. I'm getting ready for the cold weather. Please let me know. The diary hasn't reached me yet. I'll let you know as soon as it does. I hope it reaches me in time for my birthday. This makes a nice present. Dot, I'll write longer the next time. P.S. Everybody in the unit received one of those medals. Love, Dan[14]

V-MAIL

Dec. 15, 1943

Dear Dot—

*Hello, big sister. Betcha you don't know where I am. You're right,
I am in Italy. But you don't have expected me to move here. Sometime. I'm sure glad to get over here. This is where we can do the
most good. Cripes, the people over here are hard up. Their clothes
aren't even as good as the Arabs. And the towns (some of them) are
filthier than any of the ones I was in in _____. However, the
people are friendly enough and they throw out a pretty fair plate of
spaghetti. I think I'm going to like it over here. There's certainly a
lot to see. I'll write you again in a few days when I get better settled.
Bye now, Love D.*[15]

CHAPTER 28 ꧁

DANNY AND WORLD WAR II 1944

V-MAIL

Feb. 19, 1944

Dear Dot and Smitty—

Has "Junior" come yet, I hope so at least by the time this letter reaches you. Someone gave your secret away—so I've know about it for quite some time. Boy! What a pack of nieces and nephews I'm going to have by the time all you sisters finish having children. Yesterday I received a letter from Rose saying that Dale King was reported killed in action. Details though. That sort of hits home. Well, kids, I hope by the time this reaches you all will be as you wanted. Love—Dan[16]

V-MAIL

March 8, 1944

Dear Dot & Smitty—I think, if Junior doesn't hurry up and get here, my first gift to him will be a razor. He is starting out like a Clancy—late.

Our dance last Thursday was a great success. Myself and two others got pleasantly tight on vino before we went—so everything was beautiful—especially the girls.

Hope Smitty was around for the big event. That's a rugged war the people back home are fighting. Do they use real guns too!

Everything here is okay. Nice and quiet. Love—D[17]

April 10, 1944

Dear Dot—

If you don't get this letter it will be because I can't make out the address.

When I got back from Africa I found the letters from you. I'm glad you are going to visit Smitty's folks. I hope you'll be able to stay for a while. Flo & Pop would certainly love to see you. I may have a fun pix the next time I write. Getting them printed is quite a job.

My stay in Africa was a very refreshing one. Made up for a little lost time. Got stinko a few times. However, I was glad to get back.

Alborn must be quite a city. I can't find it on the map.

Dot, your description of Bonnie sure doesn't fit any new babies I've ever seen. She may have had hair and big brown eyes but I'll bet she was red as a beet and ugly. No offense; I'll love her dearly when I see her but don't send me any pictures until she can smile. I surely do like her name.

How far are you from Bedford, Ind? I have a heartthrob there. Maybe I should say I did have. I haven't heard from her for over a month so maybe she's found a new boyfriend. These fickle women!

Well, take'er cool—sis. I hope I shall see my new niece before she starts school.

Bye & Love, D[18]

Monday , Aug. 7, 1944

Dear Dot—

Your last two letters were really good. I'd rather get one like that once a month than have a V-mail every day. The picture of Bonnie Jo is very good. She is cute.

I had a perfect time on my five-day furlough. The kid I went with and myself spent the first night in Naples but that city seemed to be overcrowded with G.I.'s so we took off from Rome the next morning. It was well worth the trouble getting there. Rome is beautiful. In fact, I'd be very happy to spend the rest of my life there. I visited the Vatican, went through St. Peter's Cathedral and saw the Pope. He gave a short talk. After he finished most of the crowd left but I waited until they carried him out and just as he was about to pass me I held up several crucifixes etc. I bought and he reached down and touched my hand and blessed them. I was quite thrilled. St. Peter's Cathedral can't be described. It's just beautiful. We also saw a lot of the ruins but it would take a month or more to see everything. All the time I was there I went with a cute little girl—Romance! After nearly two years with no women you can imagine how I felt on those night walking along the banks of the Tiber with that moon shining down. Oh boy! I want to go back soon. I'm sending you a few souvenirs I picked up. They're not much though. The cross and chain for Bonnie and your crucifix were among the things I had blessed by the Pope.

I'm enclosing a couple snapshots one was taken inside the Coliseum. The ruins show up pretty well. Did you receive the snapshot of me in front of my plane?

To get back to your letter—I haven't received the package yet but I'll let you know just as soon as I do.

About going back to Butte to live. I think not. I'd rather start some-place where I don't know anyone.

When I was in Africa a few months ago I ran into a kid who was a gunner on a bomber over here. He told me he was on the same mis-sion as Dale. Said he saw the bomber blow up in the air. Keep that to yourself though cause he may have been imagining it. He had a sister living in Butte but his mother lives in Iowa, I think. I felt bad about it, but, what the heck is the difference. I'd like to take that chance too. I dread growing old a lot more than I do dying. If I get back to the States, and then have to leave again, it would be combat crew or nothing.

Well, Dot, gotta hit the hay.

So Bye for now. Love D

P.S. Your letter mailed July 28 reached me today—so there.[19]

DANNY INSIDE THE COLISEUM ON HIS FIVE-DAY FURLOUGH

Thursday, Dec. 21, 1944

Dear Dot—

Haven't heard from you for quite some time-but then I haven't heard from practically anyone so I guess I'll receive a lot of letters one of these days. I hope mine are getting to you okay.

Did I tell you in my letter that I received a package from you? Thanks a lot. Gee, in the last four days I've received 9 packages. That's what being in the army does for you. I hope that I'll be able to do some shopping next year—that is back in the States. I hate not being able to send something in return for everything I've received. You should see our food closet. All the men in the house wrote similar letters to their folks asking them to send food instead of cookies and candy. We have enough to last most of the winter. It's nice to be able to whip up a snack each evening before bed.

In Marg's last letter she said that Flo's children had been sick. Flo had better watch her own health. I hope Bonnie Jo is okay—you too.

I was all set to go to Rome for Christmas but not now. The squadron was going to send all Catholic men up there so they could attend special services at St. Peter's Cathedral. Guess too many of the men suddenly decided to change faiths. Anyway the deal fell through. In a way I'm sorta glad cause I'm still in debt from my last trip. But it would have been nice to spend Christmas Day in Rome. However, there is going to be a mass held in a town nearby Christmas Eve so I think I'll attend that if I can manage to stay awake that long.

Think I'll close for now Dot. Please write as often as you can. I'll write again soon. This poem (or whatever it is) was in our group weekly paper. I thought it was cute.

Love, D.[20]

DANNY AND WORLD WAR II 1945

Wednesday, Jan. 17, 1945

Dear Dot—

Excuse the delay in writing but since I got out of the hospital I've been busy most of the time or else in no mood for writing. But then I haven't been hearing from you very often lately either. I hope you're still with Smitty. In fact I hope his orders will change for good and he'll get a permanent job back there. It really would be nice if you and he and Bonnie could be together all the time.

Just think, Dot, if I hadn't taken that last ranking, I'd have been number two on the rotation list. I'd have been able to go home on furlough next month or wait two months and back to the States permanently. Hell, how should I have known the war would last this long. One of the kids in our house left that morning for the States to spend thirty days at home. I've been feeling rather low all day. But seriously I don't think I'd take a furlough if they offered it to me. When I get back to the States I want to stay. Probably when I do get back the war will be over and I'll be able to stay.

Well, Dot, there's nothing new to write about so guess I'll close for now and hope to hear from you soon.

Love,

D[21]

Saturday, Jan. 27, 1945

Dear Dot-

Had a letter from you yesterday dated Dec. 28. Glad to hear you all had a nice Christmas. It was nice that you could all be together. I received quite a few letters yesterday—six to be exact and that's damn good for me. Bob Osier is now in the Philippines. Also had a letter from Capt. Jim Bertoglio. He's in Germany. I'll bet things are hot where he is. From the sound of the news that must be a rugged war going on up there. Ed Bartolleti wrote to me too. The first letter I've had from him since I joined the army. I guess he is getting ready to leave the States too. Bat is also on the shipping list. The old high-school gang is really spread out around the world. I hope it won't be too long before we can all have a reunion.

It looks again as though this campaign is just about finished. I'm really anxious to find out what's going to happen when it does end. However, my guess isn't very optimistic. I believe we'll go to china or somewhere in that neck-of-the woods.

Well, Dot, gotta close now. Write soon.

Love,

D.[22]

Saturday, Feb. 17, 1945

Dear Dot-

Had a letter from Flo a short while back telling me that Smitty is heading overseas. However, I'll wait till I hear from you before I believe it. Dot, I think you'd be smart to go home if he does leave the States. You'd probably be happier back there. I told Flo to let you have whatever money you'll need.

Tonite, I'm sergeant of the guard and all I have to do is sit in the orderly room until midnite. Good time to get caught up on my correspondence. However, I sure feel low. I suppose you heard about Jim Bertoglio being killed in action. It makes me so goddamned mad when I think of all the years he spent preparing himself for something so fine as that. Then to make matters worse, his wife is going to have a baby this month. I have to write a letter to his folks but I sure don't know what to say.

Dot, I'll write again soon. There's really nothing to write about.

Bye for now [23]

April 1, 1945

Dear Dot—

Well, I've written two V-mails to you so guess I'd better write a real letter for a change. Tonite I'm pulling sergeant of the guard—all I have to do is sit in the orderly room until midnite so I decided to catch up on my letter writing. This makes my fifteenth letter. No, I'm not putting the family last. It's just that I know I'll always write to you and the rest. It's those other letters that I've been putting off for the past six months that I decided to get off my chest. Oh, yes, I wrote to Smitty, too. I've been meaning to ever since I got his address. I told him not too try to make a hero out of himself that you'd love him even if he didn't have any medals. I really do think, Dot, that almost by the time you receive this letter that it will be over, and then you can stop worrying. Gee, I hope they'll turn around and send him right back home.

Well, Dot, this is all for now. Will write again soon.

Love.

D.[24]

V-MAIL

Dear Dot—Your V-Mail of April 12 reached me yesterday. This business of writing letters is getting darn hard for me. I'll be glad when I get home and won't have to write anymore. If something interesting would happen around here that I could write about, I wouldn't mind. Hope you'll be going home soon. Why don't you try to get Bundy's apartment? Be sure to take any money you need. Flo will let you have it. Bye for now.

Love, D[25]

V-MAIL

Dear Dot—Have had several letters from you in the past week. I'm glad to hear that you had news of Smitty. Flo sent me a letter that he wrote them. I'll drop a line to him one of these days. I was rather hoping he'd be shipped to Italy. I'd like to have seen him. However, I think France is a better place to be. Don't go worrying yourself to death now. This war is going to wind up one of these days. At least I hope so. Take it easy. I'll write again soon. Love D.[26]

PART VII
CHAPTER 30 ♫

THE SOLDIERS COME HOME

The gathering in Butte included Danny, Bob Osier, and Albert Ciabattari. They sorely missed their great friend, Jim Bertoglio, who had been killed in combat in Germany, one of many of Butte's own who would not return from the war. For those who did return, homecoming centered on Meaderville, with dinner at the Rocky Mountain Café. Danny loved their delicious fried chicken, while Bob and Albert favored the spaghetti and raviolis. The men enjoyed fried celery as an appetizer while they sipped bourbon and laughed about old times in high school. Reliving boyhood memories helped them forget what they had seen at war, scenes they wanted to forget for the rest of their lives.

Bob and Albert reupped in the army. Bob and his soon-to-be wife, Mary, were leaving for Japan. The Orient, as Danny forecast in a war letter to Dot, was going to be a hot spot for some time. Albert and his wife, Pat, were stationed for a time in California. Danny wanted to stay in Montana, but wasn't sure he wanted to be in Butte. Flo, his eldest sister, and her family were there, but Marg and her husband, Harry, were in California, as was Adeline, who was still single. Dot had married Smitty and lived in Alborn, Illinois. Uprooted by the war, Danny now pondered where his life was headed.

The answer came from an unexpected direction. An old friend from Butte, Dick Gamwell, invited a Helena girl, Ann Dolan, over to dinner at the Rocky Mountain Café. Dick invited Danny to tag along. It turned out that Dick's charms were no match for Danny's sense of humor, and before long, Danny and Ann planned to marry. Ann worked at the Internal Revenue Service in Helena, and she arranged an interview for Danny. He got the job, and then met the very large Dolan clan. He was in the midst of an all-Irish family. Ann had seven brothers (Charles died as an infant), and the six lads, mostly strapping football players, gave Dan, as they called him, a hard time for being "English" due to his Welsh background. Dan rolled with their jests, and savored being spoiled by Ann's mother, Nanny. He had missed out on his mother's love, but Nanny made up for it. In turn, she enjoyed his humor and joy for life.

Like most of the men and women back from war, Danny and Ann lost no time starting a family; babies came fast and frequently. They moved to Great Falls, where the first child, Colleen, was born, but Ann missed her large family too much, and back to Helena they went, never to move again. Two sons were born within sixteen months: Daniel and Dennis, known as Dan and Din. Some seven years later, a baby sister, Terrie, was welcomed to the family. Ann's brothers and two sisters were soon busy with families of their own, rapidly doubling, then tripling, the size of the Dolan clan.

Danny's job at the Internal Revenue Service kept him busy even at night and on weekends, but he found time to volunteer at Saint Joseph's Orphanage, where his father had lived after his mother's death. Danny knew too well how lonely children in an orphanage could be. He took Colleen, Dan, and Din with him out to St. Joseph's where they visited and talked with the children who were working in the barn with the animals.

The annual Turkey Shoot on the Sunday prior to Thanksgiving was a huge event in Helena to support St. Joseph's Orphanage. All of the Clancys attended the events and the dinner the nuns put on for the supporters and the children in the home. Danny could never forget finding his father's name in the books, nor could he forget the kindness shown to him when he lived at the Paul Clark Home. Eight decades had passed since John and Margret John first ventured across the Atlantic and set foot on American soil. Welsh and Irish heritage intertwined in the four generations that struggled for a toehold on the richest hill on Earth, enduring against the odds, and finally thriving under the big sky.

NOTES ♪

FOREWORD

1. Thomas, Dylan, from *Under Milk Wood* copyright ©1952 by Dylan Thomas. Reprinted by permission of New Directions Publishing Corp., 1.

CHAPTER 1

1. Dorothy Sutherland, *Enchantment of the World: Wales* (Chicago: Children's Press, 1987), 20.

CHAPTER 2

1. "The Cornish in Butte," *Butte Heritage Cookbook* (Butte: Artcraft Printers Co., 1976), 13.

2. Kathleen Cook, "Finn Town," *Butte Heritage Cookbook* (Butte: Artcraft Printers Co., 1976), 29.

3. "Butte's Little Ireland," *Butte Heritage Cookbook* (Butte: Artcraft Printers Co., 1976), 85.

4. Andrea Ciabattari, "Meaderville," *Butte Heritage Cookbook* (Butte: Artcraft Printers Co., 1976), 99.

5. Alan Goddard, "French in Butte," *Butte Heritage Cookbook* (Butte: Artcraft Printers Co., 1976), 41.

6. "Lebanese Colony," *Butte Heritage Cookbook* (Butte: Artcraft Printers Co., 1976), 129.

7. Brenda Palagi, "The Welsh," *Butte Heritage Cookbook* (Butte: Artcraft Printers Co., 1976), 194.

8. Vernetta Kommers, "Chinese," *Butte Heritage Cookbook* (Butte: Artcraft Printers Co., 1976), 141.

9. *Copper Camp* (Helena: Riverbend Publishing, 2002), 120.

10. Ibid.

11. Ciabattari, "Meaderville," 99.

12. Ibid., 117.

13. "Bocce," Eddie Bauer Sportscraft, Ltd., Official Rule book, 4-5.

14. Ciabattari, "Meaderville," 100.

15. Sutherland, *Enchantment ... Wales*, 95.

16. Butte-Silver Bow Arts Chateau, "Fact Sheet."

CHAPTER 3

1. Sutherland, *Enchantment ... Wales*, 94.

CHAPTER 4

1. Palagi, "The Welsh," 193.

2. Sutherland, *Enchantment ... Wales*, 58.

3. Palagi, "The Welsh," 194.

CHAPTER 5

1. C. B. Glasscock, *The War of the Copper Kings: Builders of Butte and the Wolves of Wall Street* (Helena: Riverbend Publishing, 2002), 84.
2. Ibid., 38.
3. Ibid., 141.
4. *Copper Camp,* 297.
5. Ibid., 131.
6. Ibid., 36.
7. "The Paul Clark Home," *The Daily Inter Mountain,* November 17, 1900, 4.
8. Glasscock, *The War of the Copper Kings,* 92.

CHAPTER 6

1. *Butte, Montana ... The Greatest Copper Mining District in the World,* (New York: Thompson Investment Co., 1899), 6.
2. Glasscock, *The War of the Copper Kings,* 78-79.
3. Ibid., 123.
4. *Copper Camp,* 45.
5. Glasscock, *The War of the Copper Kings,* 136.
6. Ibid., 218.
7. Joseph Kinsey Howard, *Montana: High, Wide, and Handsome* (New York: Yale Press 1943), 79.
8. Glasscock, *The War of the Copper Kings,* 262.
9. Ibid., 263.

CHAPTER 7

1. *Copper Camp,* 77-78.
2. Ibid., 83.
3. Ibid., 119.

CHAPTER 8

1. George Wesley Davis, *Sketches of Butte* (Boston: The Cornhill Company, 1921), 57.

CHAPTER 9

1. *Copper Camp,* 208.

CHAPTER 11

1. David Clement, Butte, Montana, Cemetery Record, 1912. Butte Archives.

CHAPTER 14

1. *Copper Camp,* 123-24.

CHAPTER 15

1. Davis, *Sketches of Butte,* 41.
2. *Copper Camp,* 272.
3. Davis, *Sketches of Butte,* 78.
4. Ibid., 38-39.

CHAPTER 16

1. Adeline Clancy Todd, letter to author, August 17, 1995, 6.
2. Sutherland, *Enchantment ... Wales,* 18.
3. *Copper Camp,* 304.
4. Ibid., 63.
5. Ibid., 64.
6. Ibid., 65.
7. Ibid., 65.
8. Ibid., 66-67.
9. Ibid., 66.
10. Ibid., 66.

CHAPTER 17

1. "Make All Efforts to Find Mannus [*sic*] Duggan," *The Butte Miner,* June 11, 1917, 1.
2. "Thrilling Tales of Miners Who Sought Refuge in Crosscut," *The Butte Miner,* June 11, 1917, 1.
3. Ibid.

4. *"The Granite Mountain Mine Memorial—Final Letters and Sermon,"* 9/19/13 http://minememorial.org/history/letters-and-sermon.htm.

5. "Make All Efforts to Find Mannus [*sic*] Duggan," *The Butte Miner*, June 11, 1917, 1.

6. *"The Granite Mountain Mine,"* 9/19/13, http://minememorial.org/history/letters-and-sermon.htm.

7. "Public Morgue Established at Mine," *The Butte Miner*, June 12, 1917, 1.

8. "People of Missoula Are Sending Flowers," *The Butte Miner*, June 12, 1917, 1.

CHAPTER 18

1. "Armed Vigilantes Lynch I.W. W. Leader," *The Butte Miner*, August 2, 1917, 1.

2. "Act Branded As Devilish," *The Butte Miner*, August 2, 1917, 8.

3. Ibid.

CHAPTER 20

Davis, *Sketches,* 159.

CHAPTER 21

1. "Chong Sing Mysteriously Shot," *The Butte Miner*, October 15, 1921.

2. "Tong Gunmen Slay Victim and Get Away," *The Butte Miner*, February 13, 1922.

3. "All Butte Now In Chinese Tong War," *The Butte Miner*, Feb. 17, 1922.

4. "Nation-Wide Tong War Started Here Is Ended By Pact," *The Butte Miner*, June 24, 1922.

CHAPTER 23

1. Clancy Todd, 6-7.

2. Ibid.

CHAPTER 25

1. *Maroon,* 1935.

2. Clancy Todd, 3.

CHAPTERS 26, 27, 28, 29

1. Daniel John Clancy, letter to Pop, July 5, 1942.

2. Daniel John Clancy, letter to Dot, Aug. 20, 1942.

3. Ibid., Aug. 29, 1942.

4. Ibid., Oct. 29, 1942.

5. Ibid., Dec. 9, 1942.

6. Ibid., Jan. 5, 1943.

7. Ibid., Jan. 8, 1943.

8. Ibid., Jan. 20, 1943.

9. Ibid., Feb. 23, 1943.

10. Ibid., April 4, 1943.

11. Ibid., June 7, 1943.

12. Ibid., Sept. 2, 1943.

13. Ibid., Sept. 9, 1943.

14. Ibid., V-Mail, Oct. 7, 1943.

15. Ibid., Dec. 15, 1943.

16. Ibid., V-Mail, Feb. 19, 1944.

17. Ibid., March 8, 1944.

18. Ibid., April 10, 1944.

19. Ibid., Aug. 7, 1944.

20. Ibid., Dec. 21, 1944.

21. Ibid., Jan. 17, 1945.

22. Ibid., Jan. 27, 1945.

23. Ibid., Feb. 17, 1945.

24. Ibid., April 1, 1945.

25. Ibid., V-Mail.

26. Ibid., V-Mail.

BIBLIOGRAPHY ♫

"Bocce," Eddie Bauer Sportscraft, Ltd., Official Rule book, 4-5. Reprinted Courtesy of Eddie Bauer LLC.

Butte Heritage Cookbook (Butte: Artcraft Printers Co., 1976). Permission.

... Butte, Montana ... The Greatest Copper Mining District in the World (New York: Thompson Investment Co., 1899), 6.

"Butte-Silver Bow Arts Chateau." Fact Sheet.

Ciabattari McCormick, Andrea. "The Italians," *Butte Heritage Cookbook.* (Butte: Artcraft Printers Co., 1976), 99. Permission.

Cook, Kathleen. "Finn Town," *Butte Heritage Cookbook* (Butte: Artcraft Printers Co., 1976), 29.

Copper Camp. (Helena: Riverbend Publishing, 2002), 36, 77-78, 83, 119-120, 123-124, 131, 208, 272, 297, 304. Permission.

"David Clement." Butte, Montana, Cemetery Record. Butte Archives.

Davis, George Wesley. *Sketches of Butte* (Boston: The Cornhill Company 1921), 47, 57, 78, 133, 159.

"Faro," *The Encyclopedia Britannica* (New York: 1929), 97.

"Finnish Finn Town," *Butte Heritage Cookbook* (Butte: Artcraft Printers Co., 1976), 29.

Glasscock, *The War of the Copper Kings: Builders of Butte and the Wolves of Wall Street* (Helena: Riverbend Publishing, 2002), 78-79, 123, 136, 218, 262. Permission.

Goddard, Alan. "French in Butte," *Butte Heritage Cookbook* (Butte: Artcraft Printers Co., 1976), 42.

The Granite Mountain Memorial, Butte, Montana, 9/19/13. http://minememorial.org/history/letters-and-sermon.htm.

Howard, Joseph Kinsey. *Montana: High, Wide, and Handsome* (New York: Yale Press), 79.

"The Irish," *Butte Heritage Cookbook.* (Butte: Artcraft Printers Co., 1976), 85.

Kommers, Vernetta. "Oriental Chinese," *Butte Heritage Cookbook.* (Butte: Artcraft Printers Co., 1976), 141.

"Lebanese Colony," *Butte Heritage Cookbook.* (Butte: Artcraft Printers Co., 1976), 129.

Letter, Adeline Clancy Todd, August 17, 1995, 3, 6, 7.

Letter, Bonny Hemmert, June 15, 2000.

Maroon. Butte, 1935, 10.

Palagi, Brenda. "The Welsh," *Butte Heritage Cookbook.* (Butte: Artcraft Printers Co., 1976), 194.

Sutherland, Dorothy, *The Enchantment of the World: Wales,* (Chicago: Children's Press, 1987), 18, 20, 58, 94, 95. Permission.

Thomas, Dylan, from *Under Milk Wood,* copyright ©1952 by Dylan Thomas. Reprinted by permission of New Directions Publishing Corp. *Under Milk Wood* (New York: New Directions Books), Permission.

INDEX

Cigliani, Charlie- 76, 102, 107

Cigliani, Elroy- 102, 103, 107

Cigliani, Leonard- 102, 103, 107

Claddah "Hookers"- 30

Claddagh Ring- 29

Claddagh Village- 29

Clancy, Adeline (Hattie) Davis- 4, 5, 23-28, 44-48, 53, 54, 56-59, 61-67, 71, 72, 75, 76, 79, 81, 84, 91-94, 99

Clancy, Adeline Todd- 5, 99-104, 110, 114, 142

Clancy, Colleen Hansen- 142

Clancy, Daniel John Sr.- 5, 36, 41- 62, 65, 66, 75-84, 89-94, 99-105, 111, 113, 116, 123, 124

Clancy, Daniel John (Danny) Jr.- 5, 7, 91, 92, 99, 101-143

Clancy, Daniel John Jr.- 142

Clancy, Dennis- 142

Clancy, Dorothy Smith- 5, 62, 65, 71, 72, 81-83, 92, 99, 102, 103, 107, 113-139, 142

Clancy, Ellen Casey Newman- 5, 36, 41, 46, 62

Clancy, Florence (Flo) Schneller- 5, 62, 63, 65, 71, 72, 81-82, 92, 99, 102, 103, 107, 117, 123, 130, 139, 142

Clancy, John Daniel- 5, 29-31, 33, 35, 37, 41-43, 46

Clancy, Margaret (Marg) Page- 5, 59-68, 71, 72, 81, 82, 92, 99, 102, 103, 107, 114, 118, 142

Clancy, Terrie Casey- 142

Clark, Charles Walker- 19

Clark, Katherine Quinn Roberts- 19, 20

Clark, Paul- 20, 32, 33

Clark, W. A. Mansion- 33

Clark, William A.- 30-33, 38, 75, 105

Clement, David- 25, 59

Clement, David Jr.- 25, 59

Clement baby (unnamed)- 25

Cobban, A.- 86

Cofrestr Deuluaidd- 11

Cofrestr Teuluaidd- 12

Columbia Gardens- 30, 44, 46, 81, 82, 104, 108

Columbia School of Mines- 30, 33

Colusa- 30

Comique-36

Comstock Mine- 31

Conscription Act- 108

Copper Kings- 30, 31, 86

Coracles- 10, 22

Cornish- 17

County Cavan, Ireland- 31

County Galway- 29

"Cousin Jack" pasties- 47

"Cowboy Chinaman"- 96

Cynghanedd- 28

D

Daly, Marcus- 30, 31, 33, 51

"Dardanelles" - 78

Davis, Billy- 4, 62

Davis, Clara- 4, 62, 101

Davis, Ernesta- 4, 122

Davis, Florence Cigliani- 4, 25, 27, 47, 57, 83, 99, 100, 102-04

Davis, Gordon- 4, 62

Davis, Joyce- 4

Davis, Janet- 4

Davis, Joan- 4, 62, 83

Davis, Margaret John- 4, 10, 12, 14, 19, 21-25, 45, 47, 53, 54, 56, 67, 68, 71, 72, 83, 91, 99, 103, 107

Davis, Rose- 4, 62, 83, 129

Davis, Rosemary- 4, 62, 83

ACKNOWLEDGMENT: ᕲ

To families everywhere whose life stories guide and sustain all who follow.

I would like to thank all the Clancy cousins who shared photographs and especially a cousin I have yet to meet in person, Bonny Hemmert, who provided the John family history and the beautiful Cofrestr Deuluaidd (Lloyd-John Marriage Certificate) and Cofrestr Teuluaidd (John Family Tree). Thank you to early readers: Dan and Gilda Clancy, Dennis Clancy, Terrie Clancy, Shelley Hansen Heimlich, Mary Jane Page Hellebust, Lynn Todd Loving, Dannette Schneller Pirkl, and Ed Smith.

Destination: Butte, Montana, came to life through the careful first edit by Andrea Ciabattari McCormick. Thank you to Sweetgrass Books staff: Kathy Springmeyer, Director of Publications, for guidance in the publishing process and for your care with the old photographs; Will Harmon, Senior Editor, you enthusiastically encouraged more details, and Kelli Street, for the attractive design.

Thank you to Mary Patchett for permission to use her husband Tom Patchett's art to grace the cover and entice those who loved the Columbia Gardens to pick up my book. Mary said she had not seen the art before, but I found the drawing many years ago at an antique sale at the Helena Civic Center.

Thank you to my husband, Alec, and my two beautiful children, Lucy and Eamon, and my favorite grandson, Gus Darty.

ABOUT THE AUTHOR ᴥ

Colleen Clancy Hansen holds a bachelor's degree in Secondary Education with an English major and a speech/drama minor, and a master's degree in the Art of Teaching. She retired after teaching secondary English for twenty-five years.

Always encouraging students to publish their work, Colleen was on the *Signatures from Big Sky* board to select Montana students' writing for inclusion in the magazine. She helped edit *Pannings/Writings on the Wall,* a Helena High School magazine, for twelve years. Then she began to enter writing competitions and was awarded eighth place in inspirational writing in the 82nd annual *Writers Digest* competition and honorable mention in the 78th *Writers Digest* competition for the poem, "To a Grandmother, Adeline, I Never Knew." She was invited to read the poem at Carroll College's Literary Festival in 2010. The poem is the basis for *Destination: Butte, Montana.*

Alec Hansen, Colleen's husband of forty-three years, is the director of the Montana League of Cities and Towns (he represents all 130 cities and towns). They have two children: Lucy, a family law attorney in Missoula, and Eamon, who graduated from Carroll College in public relations and communication. Lucy's son Gus is a six-year-old bibliophile.

www.ingramcontent.com/pod-product-compliance
Lightning Source LLC
Chambersburg PA
CBHW072101040426
42334CB00041B/1819